M000266888

SEA SALT

This book is dedicated to the friends and family who
sit round our kitchen table and feast with us.

SEA SALT

A PERFECTLY SEASONED COOKBOOK

~

The Lea-Wilson Family

with Anna Shepherd

Photography by Liz and Max Haarala Hamilton

WHITE LION PUBLISHING

Contents

Cynnwys

An introduction to sea salt

Cyflwyniad i halen môr

An unparalleled ingredient

Salt is the single most important ingredient in the kitchen, and being able to season properly is what separates a good cook from an excellent one. A crisp and tender chicken Caesar salad bound together by a balanced, umami dressing; a bright and fresh margarita, each sip leaving salt on your lips; delicate fritto misto, coated in seasoned batter and finished with flakes of sea salt are all impossible to imagine left unsalted. Simply put, a salted tomato tastes more of tomato. Deeper, richer, more mouth-watering, and when it comes to cooking, salt is utterly transformative – to texture, flavour, even, as the author and presenter of *Salt, Fat, Acid, Heat*, Samin Nosrat points out, to aroma. Take an unctuous French onion soup, for example. Salt added at the beginning draws the water out of the onions when they first start cooking, concentrating their flavour, then salt added to the broth balances and brightens it, and finally, seasoning the croutons properly finishes the bowl with a savoury note. It even smells better.

Of course, there is the bounty of foods that are preserved with the help from salt – from mackerel and gravadlax, to capers nestled among salt crystals and olives swimming in brine.

Sweet dishes too, sing when salt is added, rescuing them from being that bit too much. Picture the richest chocolate dessert, topped by glossy ganache and finished with the merest hint of a few flakes.

We can think of few ingredients that change dishes in the same way as salt does. What would life be without a smooth caramel punctuated by salt crystals, a perfectly cured bacon rasher, or a warm handful of glistening, salted potato crisps? This is why we have collated some of our favourite recipes – to show how proper seasoning can elevate everyday classics, as well add to some more unexpected dishes. Give this book to people who say they don't use, or (heaven forbid) say they don't like, salt; whether raw or cooked, properly seasoned food is a revelation.

Different types of salt

Not all salts are made equal. Despite having the advantage of being cheap and rarely clumping together, table salt is often laden with anticaking agents that can bring their own bitter flavour to your food. Rock salt adds a texture suggested by its name, which works in some dishes but not others (and requires mining to extract).

The salt we broadly recommend is (you guessed it) sea salt. We always have at least one finer flake and one with larger crunchy crystals in our kitchen, both on the table and near the cooker. We refer to them in our recipes as finer flaked and flaked sea salt. The former dissolves quickly, making it good when cooking, while the flaked variety offers crunches of salt, which are perfect for finishing dishes.

Then there are the flavoured varieties. You will find everything from citrus-scented sea salt to scorching chilli flavoured. It's best to add these at the end of cooking to maximise their flavour. We favour the classic varieties – celery sea salt in a Bloody Mary is a thing of beauty and a few flakes of oak-smoked sea salt on a boiled free-range egg is a joy to behold. Another favourite is a homemade citrus salt – amazing on new potatoes or a tomato salad. Add the zest of a lemon to a tablespoon of salt, and rub with clean hands to release the amazing aromatic oils.

Our vanilla sea salt is a homage to a family trip taken to French Polynesia – it was the second flavour we released, and we have been selling it steadily, since 1998. If you'd prefer to make it yourself then here is an idea of how. We can't call it a recipe in all honesty but it's a lovely luxury to have in the cupboard. All you need to get started are fairtrade vanilla pods and some finer flaked sea salt. Start with one pod to around 50g/1¾oz of salt and decide how intense you want to go.

Using a sharp knife, split the vanilla pods lengthways down the centre and scrape out as many of the precious seeds as you can. Using clean fingers, rub it into a small bowl of salt to mix as evenly as possible. In general we like a lot of vanilla, but it's precious and therefore expensive. Keep the salt in a sealed jar and pop the empty pod in there to carry on infusing. This salt is also delicious on shellfish, delicate white fish or cookies.

How much salt to use

Salt has been vilified to such an extent that many people fear it in any quantity at all. Far be it for us to offer health advice, but it's worth pointing out that our bodies physically need salt to function. Undoubtedly, as with most things, too much is bad for you, but when you cook from scratch, it's easier to know how much salt you are actually eating.

Perhaps the simplest (and best) piece of advice this book will have to offer is you is this: to add salt at different stages of the cooking process, and to keep tasting your endeavours. Generally speaking, adding a small amount of salt at every stage will have more effect than adding a handful at the end. It will give you far more refined results and mean you use less overall.

Our story + process

Our life has centred around sea salt – making it, perfecting it and travelling the world selling it – for over 20 years.

Back in 1997 we were running an aquarium that we had started as students. It showcased the wide variety of marine life to be found around our small but beloved Welsh island of Anglesey. By law we had to pay The Crown Estate for the seawater that we extracted, as the Queen owns the coastline. Much to our surprise, we were able to breed notoriously fussy seahorses, in large part due to the purity of the water they were living in.

When tourism numbers began to drop, and times were tough, we began to think about what else we could do with that sparkling clean seawater, so one weekend, we made our first batch of sea salt in a saucepan on our old Aga. What followed was an intensive few years of trial and error, travelling to Japan to see how they made it, sneaking into chemistry lectures at the local university, and ultimately, a lot of fine-tuning. Nowadays, while we have a consistent process, we are still learning every day. The sea and its mineral content is an ever-changing beast.

We use seawater drawn from the Menai Strait around Anglesey. Before the water even reaches our saltcote (an old French word for a building by the sea), it has already passed through two natural filters: a mussel bed and a sandbank. We then gently heat the seawater in a vacuum so it boils at a lower temperature. Gradually, the water releases steam and turns into a very salty brine. When the concentration of the salt in the water is high enough, we release it into shallow crystallisation tanks and leave it there overnight to allow the incredibly beautiful sea salt crystals to form. Every single flake is then harvested by hand before being rinsed in brine until it shines.

While the majority of our sea salt is kept plain, some of it is blended with a range of the finest ingredients to make our seasoned range – chilli salt, vanilla salt, celery salt, to name a few, or kiln-smoked onsite over oak chips to create our own bespoke smoked range.

As of 2022, we take great pride in supplying some of the world's best restaurants. Our products are used both by Michelin-starred chefs and home cooks. We are also an ingredient in Pipers Crisps as well as in Green and Black's

chocolate. We have supplied royal weddings, Olympic ceremonies and even seasoned Barack Obama's favourite caramels.

Our home

This wild island of Ynys Môn (Anglesey) off the northwest coast of Wales that we call home is characterised by storybook coastlines, seemingly endless dunes, green, green grass and, most importantly for us, incredibly clean seas. Halen Môn (literally 'Anglesey salt') was born out of a real love for Ynys Môn, its people, landscape and unmatched natural resource.

So, in 2014, when our sea salt joined the likes of Champagne, Parma ham and Melton Mowbray Pork Pies to have Protected Designation of Origin status, it felt surprisingly emotional for us. We have always been proud of where our sea salt comes from and this accolade legally recognises Halen Môn as having unique qualities due to our geographical location as well as the way we make it. Under the EU's Protected Food Name scheme, certain food and drink products receive Europe-wide legal protection against imitation and misuse, which means that no other company or country can 'pass off' their product under the quality Halen Môn/Anglesey Sea Salt name.

Our food philosophy

Sustainability has been at the core of our business for as long as we have been in it, so it makes sense that it is fundamental to our eating habits, too. For us, this means eating seasonally, eating less meat, supporting local producers wherever possible and also (and we know this is a luxury) growing much of our food in our kitchen garden. Of course, we use lemons, spices and more from further

afield, as to us, these ingredients bring their irreplaceable sunshine with them. We take great care to buy organic and/or fairtrade depending on the product for example, we recommend using organic or, at the minimum, free-range eggs for the recipes in this book. Knowing where our food comes from is a big thing for us as it's integral to our own business.

Eating seasonally means far more than avoiding supermarket asparagus in winter – it means choosing ingredients, be they fat blackberries or luminescent rhubarb stalks, when they are at their very best. It is better for the world and it tastes so much better, too.

Like many modern families, within ours we all have different attitudes to meat and fish. When we do eat it, it is organic and local, but many of our suppers celebrate vegetables and we give them as much attention, seasoning and preparation as we do meat. Many of the techniques traditionally associated with meats – brining and curing – can also bring a new dimension to vegetables, as we hope this book demonstrates.

Becoming part of the UK speciality food community over the years has been a genuine pleasure. Food festivals are among the highlights of our calendar year, when we swap our sea salt for vine-scented tomatoes, handmade samosas, sourdough loaves, Welsh salamis and exquisite chocolates. We have learned that we really vote with our wallets. Buying local produce from people who care about making it means they can continue to produce products ethically, look after their environment and pay staff fairly.

While, realistically, we do buy from supermarkets, we consciously support local shops and growers – our local farmshop, Hooton's in Brynsiencyn, is a regular destination, as is a fishmonger on the Llyn Peninsula, and our butcher's Swains in Menai Bridge (who, incidentally, was our very first customer).

The pleasure of eating

It is difficult to overstate the love we have for good food. Making, growing, cooking and eating it. Our family is the sort that discusses what to have for lunch long before breakfast is over. Weekends are more about the meals than what we do between them. Whole holidays are planned around a single restaurant, market or food producer, and the aisles of a supermarket abroad bring us a joy unparalleled by much else.

We hope that this book communicates some of the joy we find in food and celebrates the ingredient that has been so central to all our lives. We have worked with a talented chef and friend, Anna Shepherd, to develop and hone many of the recipes in the following pages, all of which use sea salt to make them taste their very best. There are feasts from our family table, simple suppers and lunches we have cooked for special customers who have travelled from all over the world. Not to mention some suggestions for drinks and sensational desserts to celebrate the versatility of sea salt (see page 193 to go straight to the sweet stuff) as well as new ideas, old favourites and even some secrets behind the bestselling dishes from our outdoor café menu. We hope you enjoy it.

The Lea-Wilson family
Ynys Môn/Anglesey, 2021

RAW

SEASONING

SEIGIAU

AMRWD

Celeriac remoulade with pumpkin seeds

Remoulade celeriac gyda hadau pwmpen

 30 minutes, plus 1 hour standing

4

Celeriac remoulade is a classic. The very taste of French holidays, and, in our opinion, not made enough on UK shores. Obviously homemade mayonnaise takes this up a notch, but it's not something we make outside special occasions in our house, so we like to use yogurt for a lighter taste. Salting the celeriac for an hour or so cures the vegetable before you dress it, seasoning it from the inside out, and helping it retain that satisfying crunch.

½ celeriac, peeled

1 tsp finer flaked sea salt, plus a pinch

2 tbsp Greek yogurt or mayonnaise (p.38)

1 tbsp wholegrain mustard

1 tsp apple cider vinegar

Freshly ground black pepper

To finish

50g/1¾oz pumpkin seeds, toasted

Olive oil for drizzling

Small bunch of parsley, leaves picked and finely chopped

Ideally, use a mandolin to matchstick the celeriac, but if you don't have one, begin by finely slicing the celeriac to a thickness of 2–3mm/ ¹⁄₁₆–⅛ in, then slice across the celeriac to form thin matchsticks.

Put the celeriac into a large bowl and sprinkle over the 1 teaspoon salt. Using clean hands, massage the salt into the celeriac, then leave to stand at room temperature for about 1 hour.

Meanwhile, prepare the dressing. Put the yogurt, mustard and vinegar into a medium bowl and use a fork to mix together. Add a good grind of black pepper.

Once the celeriac has finished curing, submerge it in a bowl of cold water, then rinse thoroughly under cold running water for about 5 minutes. Drain in a colander and pat dry with a clean tea towel.

Dress the celeriac with the vinaigrette, taste, then season again, if needed.

Put the seeds into a small bowl, drizzle with a little olive oil and the remaining pinch of salt and mix until combined.

Scatter the chopped parsley and pumpkin seeds over the remoulade and serve with 12 slices of air-dried ham and crusty white bread as a treat for lunch or to start a dinner.

Beetroot carpaccio with roasted lemon

Carpaccio betys gyda lemon rhost

This is no ordinary salad. The salt transforms both the beets and lemon here – the former are given a kind of soft cure and the latter salted, sugared and roasted to bring a whole new sherbety flavour to this sour fruit. When selecting beetroot for this, choose vegetables that feel firm under the skin. Unwaxed lemons are especially important here as you are eating the whole fruit. To make this into a more substantial meal, serve with cooked grains and griddled slices of halloumi.

For the salad

400g/14oz beetroot (we like to use a mixture of purple, golden and candy), peeled

1 round shallot, finely diced or ½ banana shallot, finely diced

Juice of 1 lemon

2 tbsp extra virgin olive oil, plus extra for drizzling

1 heaped tsp caster sugar

1 tsp finer flaked sea salt

50g/1¾oz peppery leaves, such as rocket or watercress

Flaked sea salt

For the almond caper crumble

1 lemon

¼ tsp caster sugar

¼ tsp finer flaked sea salt

2 tbsp extra virgin olive oil

50g/1¾oz soft white breadcrumbs

½ small bunch of parsley, leaves picked and roughly chopped

½ small bunch of dill, leaves picked and roughly chopped

30g/1oz almonds, toasted and roughly chopped

1 tbsp baby capers, drained

 40 minutes, plus 30 minutes marinating

4

Preheat the oven to 200°C/180°C fan/400°F/Gas 6.

Line a large baking sheet with baking paper.

Slice the beetroot finely on a mandolin into a medium bowl. Add the shallot, lemon juice, olive oil, sugar and finer flaked salt and toss to combine. Cover and leave to marinate at room temperature for 30 minutes.

Meanwhile, make the crumble. Remove both ends of the lemon, so the flesh is visible, then cut the lemon in half around the middle. Slice one half into thin 5mm/¼in rounds and arrange the slices on the lined baking sheet in a single layer. Sprinkle with the sugar and salt and roast in the oven for 10–12 minutes until the slices are beginning to caramelise in places. Use a sharp knife to cut away the skin and white pith from the other lemon half and cut the lemon into segments by slicing the flesh between the white membrane, discarding any seeds as you go. Transfer the lemon segments to a medium bowl.

Heat the olive oil in a frying pan over a medium heat. Add the breadcrumbs and stir well to coat in the oil. Cook for 6–8 minutes, stirring frequently, until the breadcrumbs are crisp and dark golden all over. Stir in the herbs, almonds and capers and cook for another 30 seconds, then remove from the heat and transfer to the bowl with the lemon segments.

Remove the roasted lemon slices from the oven and dice them finely on a chopping board. Add these to the bowl with the lemon segments and breadcrumbs and toss to combine.

Arrange the beetroot slices on a large platter and pour over the juices and shallot pieces from the bowl. Arrange the peppery leaves over a quarter of the beetroot and drizzle with olive oil. Scatter over 2 tablespoons of the crumble mixture, then sprinkle with a pinch of flaked sea salt to season both the beetroot and leaves. Serve the carpaccio with the remaining crumble mixture in a bowl at the table for extra crunch.

Courgette with buttermilk + poppy seed dressing

Corbwmpen gyda llaeth enwyn a dresin hadau pabi

🕐 20 minutes, plus 1 hour standing

🍴 4–6 as a side

In the summer our garden overflows with courgettes, and for weeks we have to come up with ingenious ways of using them. This is my (Alison's) favourite – the dressing is gentle but a little tangy, and a spoonful of this goes well with grilled sardines or roast ham. Make this dish your own by adding soft herbs such as tarragon, or stirring in crushed garlic and a smidge of honey for sweetness. It's best eaten on the day you make it.

For the salad

3 yellow courgettes
3 green courgettes
2 tsp finer flaked
   sea salt

For the buttermilk citrus dressing

1½ tsp poppy seeds
150ml/5fl oz buttermilk
Juice of ½ lemon
Juice of ½ orange
Finely grated zest of 1 lemon
2 tbsp olive oil
A good grind of black pepper, or to taste
¼ tsp finer flaked sea salt

Carefully slice the courgettes into ribbons on a mandolin or with a 'y'-shaped vegetable peeler, being careful of your hands. Scatter the salt onto the strips, then leave them to rest in a colander placed in the sink or standing on a plate to draw some of the water out for 1 hour.

Rinse the salt off the courgettes (taste some to check you have rinsed them enough), then pat completely dry with kitchen paper. You can store them like this in the fridge in a covered dish overnight, if needed.

To make the dressing, toast the poppy seeds in a hot, dry frying pan until fragrant, then transfer to a clean jam jar with the remaining ingredients. Cover the jar with the lid and shake well to combine.

Pile the courgettes onto a platter and drizzle with the shaken dressing. Serve immediately.

Pan con tomate

Pan con tomate

 15 minutes

 4 as part of a spread

In the height of summer, we cannot think of a better breakfast, lunch or dinner than one with pan con tomate at its core. A traditional Catalan dish, it was first introduced to us by Francesc, who imports Halen Môn salt to Spain and knows more about good food and ingredients than anyone else we can think of.

1 plain ciabatta

1 garlic clove, unpeeled and halved

2–3 large, very ripe tomatoes at room temperature, halved down the middle

Extra virgin olive oil, for drizzling

Flaked sea salt

Preheat the oven to 190°C/170°C fan/375°F/Gas 5.

Start by cutting the ciabatta lengthways, arrange on a baking sheet and toast in the oven for 12–15 minutes until it has crisped up and is golden. You want the bread to be very crispy for the tomatoes and garlic to rub well on top of it.

Next, rub a halved garlic clove all over the cut side of the bread, then rub a tomato half vigorously over the bread. You want lots of the juice and seeds to stick to the cripsy bread. Repeat with the other half of the ciabatta. Drizzle with a generous amount of olive oil and add a good pinch of flaked sea salt. Serve immediately.

Gem lettuce summer rolls

Rholenni letus bach hafaidd

 30 minutes

 4–6

If you like anchovies, then this is the sauce for you. A vibrant and light lunch or starter that really celebrates the best of summer vegetables, it uses sweet lettuce leaves as the roll wrapper for added crunch. If you want to bulk it up for a supper, crumbling in some of the cured tofu on p.157 or layering in some cooked and drained rice noodles wouldn't go amiss. For meat eaters, this is a fresh and lovely accompaniment to the Chicken Wings on p.90 for a relaxed and hands-on meal.

For the anchovy dipping sauce

6 anchovy fillets in oil

85ml/3fl oz extra virgin olive oil

75ml/2½fl oz ice-cold water

1 large garlic clove, peeled

20ml/¾fl oz lemon juice

2 tbsp tightly packed soft white breadcrumbs

½ tsp maple syrup

¼ tsp curry powder

1 tsp snipped chives

Freshly ground black pepper

For the rolls

½ cucumber, cut into 1cm/½in segments

10 radishes, finely sliced into rounds

100g/3½oz mixed baby carrots, peeled and quartered

1 avocado, peeled, pitted and cut into 1cm/½in segments

Small bunch of spring onions, white and light green parts cut into thin strips

100g/3½oz mangetout, cut into 5mm/¼in lengths

Extra virgin olive oil, for drizzling

½ tsp flaked sea salt

2 heads of baby gem lettuce, leaves separated

Drain the anchovies and add to a high-speed blender with the olive oil, water, garlic, lemon juice, breadcrumbs, maple syrup and curry powder. Season generously with black pepper and blitz until a thick, pale sauce forms.

Alternatively, in a deep bowl, use a stick blender and blitz the anchovies, garlic, lemon juice and breadcrumbs to a paste with the spices. Pour in a quarter of the oil and blitz again, then follow with a quarter of the water. Continue adding the oil and water, and blitzing until it is combined, and the mixture is smooth. Stir in the maple syrup and season with black pepper.

Transfer the sauce to a bowl, cover and chill in the fridge until ready to use. The sauce can be made up to three days in advance.

When ready to serve, arrange the vegetables on a platter, drizzle over a glug of olive oil to make the vegetables glisten in places, then sprinkle over the salt. Place the lettuce on another plate.

Remove the anchovy sauce from the fridge and scatter over the chives. To construct the rolls, take 2–3 pieces of each vegetable and place in the centre of a piece of lettuce. Drizzle over 1 teaspoon of the anchovy sauce (with the rest in a bowl for dipping), then roll the leaves from the edge into the centre to secure the vegetables and eat while everything is fresh and crunchy.

Walnut tarator

 10 minutes, plus 10 minutes soaking

4–6

Some version of this creamy dip, with a similar texture to hummus, can be found throughout much of Eastern Europe and the Middle East. The walnuts are the highlight here and are given added complexity by smoked sea salt and a real punch from the garlic. Switch up the vegetables you use for dipping according to the season.

For the tarator

75g/2¾oz stale white bread

100g/3½oz walnuts, toasted

3 garlic cloves, crushed

75ml/2½fl oz extra virgin olive oil, plus extra for drizzling

1 tbsp lemon juice

2 tsp red wine vinegar

¾ tsp smoked sea salt, plus extra for sprinkling

½ tsp ground cumin

1 tbsp tahini

Pinch of ground cayenne pepper

Sprigs of dill, to garnish

For the crudités

A mixture of fresh vegetables:

Spring: asparagus, lettuce and salad leaves, radishes with leaves, peas in their pods

Summer: mangetout, fennel, new season carrots, cucumber, tomatoes

Autumn: celery, blanched beans, baby beetroot

Winter: cauliflower, chicory, blanched purple sprouting broccoli

Toasted bread or breadsticks, for dipping

To make the tarator, put the bread into a medium bowl and cover with cold water. Leave to soak for 10 minutes.

Squeeze the bread in a colander over the sink to remove as much water as possible, then transfer to a food processor with the walnuts and garlic. Mix the olive oil, lemon juice and vinegar together in a jug until the mixture looks thickened and emulsified. With the motor running, slowly pour the oil mixture into the food processor until it has all been used, then add the salt, cumin and tahini and pulse to combine. With the motor running again, slowly pour in up to 60ml/2fl oz water until a thick, smooth paste forms. Transfer to a small serving bowl and sprinkle with the cayenne and extra salt. Drizzle over 1 tablespoon of olive oil and scatter over the sprigs of dill.

Cut the vegetables into bite-sized pieces, leaving any longer vegetables like fennel and carrots long from root to tip for a variety of shapes to dip into the tarator. Arrange the vegetables on a platter with the dip in the centre and serve.

The tarator can be covered and stored in the fridge for up to three days.

A kind of Tunisian chopped salad

Math o salad mân Tiwnisaidd

 10 minutes, plus 30 minutes infusing

 4

As a younger family we used to go on holiday most years to Tunisia, to a tiny island called Kerkennah. I (Jess) could probably write a whole book on these vivid trips, but the food memories are the ones in particular technicolour. The dish that stands out though, was eaten on the back of a rather battered felucca. The skipper started a barbecue by whirling it round his head to 'get it going'. He grilled fresh sardines and served them with a filo-like pastry filled with egg and deep-fried to perfection and this delicious salad.

1 small red onion, finely chopped

350g/12oz ripest tomatoes, chopped into 2cm/¾in pieces

2 red peppers, chopped into 2cm/¾in pieces

1 green pepper, chopped into 2cm/¾in pieces

1 large cucumber, chopped into 2cm/¾in pieces

Small bunch of parsley, leaves picked and roughly chopped

2 tbsp extra virgin olive oil

½ tsp sweet smoked paprika

1 tsp flaked sea salt

Handful of feta or black olives (optional)

Put all the vegetables and parsley into a salad bowl and dress with the olive oil, paprika and salt. Taste and add more if you like. Leave the flavours to mingle for 30 minutes or so before eating.

It's lovely with a handful of feta or black olives, but just as good without, and works beautifully alongside an omelette.

Venison tartare

Tartare cig carw

 30 minutes

 2 as a main, or 4 as a starter

Venison has a bit of a reputation. It is a bit Henry VIII. A bit Balmoral. However, don't let this put you off. It's a beautiful meat, rich in flavour while being incredibly lean. The vast majority of venison is wild so it makes a great sustainable substitute for beef. There are many species of deer and they are all delicious and only subtly different, so focus on buying wild venison from a good butcher. This dish pairs the richness of venison with the classic French flavours of steak tartare. If you want to dress it up, then replace the mushroom with black truffle shavings.

1 tsp olive oil

5 shakes of Tabasco sauce, or to taste

1 tsp Dijon mustard

1 tsp mayonnaise (p.38)

Generous pinch of freshly ground
black pepper

1 tsp truffle oil

300g/10½oz trimmed loin of venison

1 shallot, finely chopped

3 tbsp finely diced cornichons

3 tbsp finely chopped capers

30g/1oz chives, finely chopped

1 medium egg yolk per serving

¼–½ tsp smoked sea salt

30g/1oz chestnut mushrooms

Sourdough toast, to serve

Put the olive oil, Tabasco, mustard, mayonnaise and black pepper together into a small bowl and whisk until combined. Truffle oils can vary hugely in intensity, so add a few drops at a time and taste until you have got the balance you are looking for. The truffle flavour should be a background note and not the main event.

Leave the dicing of the venison until the latest reasonable time before eating, then cut the meat into 5mm/¼in cubes.

To assemble the dish, mix the venison, shallots, cornichons, capers and dressing together in a large bowl. Taste once thoroughly mixed and add additional Tabasco or truffle oil, if you like.

If you have it, use a metal ring mould to portion the mixture on each serving plate to form a neat circle. Before removing the ring, add a generous topping of chives, then add the egg yolk and a big pinch of smoked salt on top. This salt is the only seasoning added, so be generous. You are aiming for a clearly defined traffic light of colours – rich red venison tartare, vibrant green chives and bright orange yolk. Remove the ring and shave the raw mushroom (a mandolin is best for this) over the dish. Serve immediately with toasted sourdough.

Note
By adding the smoked salt on top of the chives, you ensure you maintain the texture and pop of smoked flavour when it is mixed into the tartare by the lucky diner.

Cabbage + Parmesan slaw

Slô bresych a pharmesan

 20 minutes

6–8

Simply THE best treatment for a white cabbage. This is wonderful alongside everything from a roast chicken to a whole roasted cauliflower and is just as happy in a pitta with falafel, or at a barbecue next to some ribs. This is a simple recipe, but each process makes a big difference to the outcome. Massaging the cabbage in salt and lemon juice changes its character entirely, and the dressing makes it into something delicious.

1 white cabbage, about 1kg/2lb 3¼oz

1 scant tsp finer flaked sea salt, plus a pinch for sprinkling

Juice of 1 lemon (about 2 tbsp)

1 garlic clove

40g/1½oz Parmesan cheese, very finely grated, ideally on a Microplane

Small bunch of parsley, leaves picked and finely chopped

2 tbsp extra virgin olive oil

Freshly ground black pepper

Cut the cabbage into quarters through the root, so the root holds the layers of leaves intact. Use a mandolin to finely slice the cabbage into thin strips into a large bowl, stopping just before you get to the root which can be discarded as it's too tough to eat raw. Add the salt and lemon juice and, using clean hands, massage into the cabbage for 1–2 minutes until the cabbage starts to soften and has reduced in volume by a third.

Lay the garlic clove on a chopping board and press down to crush it with the side of a sharp knife. Sprinkle a pinch of salt over the garlic and roughly chop it with the knife. Continue a sequence of pressing down on the garlic, then chopping it until the garlic forms a rough paste. Alternatively, use a pestle and mortar. Add to the bowl with the cabbage, along with the Parmesan, parsley, olive oil and a generous grind of black pepper (about 40 turns of the pepper mill is about right). Toss well to combine.

Transfer to a bowl and serve. Best eaten on the day you make it.

Herbed scallop ceviche

Ceviche cregyn bylchog a pherlysiau

🕐 20 minutes, plus 4 hours freezing + resting

🍴 Serves 4 as a starter

This recipe celebrates scallops in all their glory. Look for hand-dived scallops and not dredged ones, as hand-dived scallops are better for the seabed and marine life.

6 king scallops

Juice of 4 lemons or 4 limes to give about 100ml/3½fl oz

1 tbsp caster sugar

1 tsp finer flaked sea salt

1 large red chilli, deseeded and finely chopped

2 spring onions, white and light green parts finely sliced at an angle

2 tsp extra virgin olive oil

1 handful of basil leaves, roughly torn

2 tsp snipped chives

Freshly ground black pepper

Fennel fronds, to garnish

Pat the scallops dry with kitchen paper and trim the orange roe (coral) away from the round white scallop (use the roe in fish pies or simply fry in butter and garlic and enjoy). Put all the trimmed scallops in a line on a piece of clingfilm and wrap tightly to seal, then twist the ends of the clingfilm so the scallops are tightly packed in a sausage shape. Freeze for 3 hours. This will firm the flesh, making them easier to slice thinly.

Remove the scallops from the freezer and defrost, still in the wrapping, at room temperature for 20 minutes, then unwrap the scallops and lay on a chopping board. Using a very sharp knife, slice the scallops into thin 3mm/⅛in rounds, then put the slices into a 20 x 30cm/8 x 12in tray or container in an even layer.

Put the citrus juice, sugar, salt and chilli into a jug and mix together until the sugar and salt have dissolved. Pour the mixture over the scallops and top with the spring onions. Mix with a couple of spoons to ensure every scallop is coated in the lime juice mixture, then cover and set aside at room temperature for 30 minutes, or until the scallops are opaque.

Using a fork, transfer the scallop slices to a serving platter. Mix 1 tablespoon of the marinade with the olive oil and pour over the scallops. Top with the herbs, season generously with black pepper and serve immediately.

Very good homemade butter

This is a really magical staple to make and one of those things you feel you are creating something out of nothing. You can make this in a jam jar by shaking it for a long time (about 20 minutes) until it thickens and finally separates, but it's much quicker to use a stand mixer or even a food processor with a normal blade. Unsalted butter should be eaten within a couple of days but salting it means it can be kept for 2–3 weeks.

600ml/21fl oz double cream (the best quality you can get your hands on)
Sea salt or flavourings of choice (see below)

 8–15 minutes

 Makes about 300g/10½oz

Pour the cream into a stand mixer or a food processor fitted with a blade and keep slowly churning through the whipped cream phase until it separates into butterfat and milk. You will hear the noise of the machine change as the cream thickens and finally sounds sloshy as it separates. This should take about 10 minutes depending on your machine.

Have a large bowl of ice-cold water ready nearby. Strain the butter through butter muslin over a bowl and reserve the buttermilk to use in a salad dressing (see p.23 for our courgette salad) or soda bread.

Check all the buttermilk is strained out by squeezing the butter submerged in a bowl of ice-cold water until the water is clear. If the buttermilk stays in the butter it can sour it.

Spread the butter out onto a piece of baking paper. You can sprinkle it with salt or other flavourings and roll it up like a Swiss roll, cutting it into rounds to serve, or you can mix in the seasoning so it is amalgamated as one.

Flavour variations

Anchovy
To 100g/3½oz unsalted butter, add 8 anchovy fillets drained and very finely chopped and ½–1 teaspoon lemon juice and beat well to combine.

Garlic
To 100g/3½oz unsalted butter, add 3 finely chopped garlic cloves crushed in ½ teaspoon sea salt.

Chilli
To 100g/3½oz unsalted butter, add 1 teaspoon chilli powder, ½ teaspoon Dijon mustard and ½ teaspoon finer flaked sea salt and beat well to combine. Use on steaks or butternut soup, roasted pumpkin or baked sweet potatoes.

Seaweed
To 100g/3½oz unsalted butter, take 2 teaspoons dried seaweed flakes (we usually use aonori seaweed) and toast in a hot dry frying pan until crisp and aromatic; grind to a powder in a pestle and mortar and stir through the softened butter. Add to grilled fish or grilled mushrooms.

HOT
SEASONING

SEIGIAU
POETH

Bone marrow beef burgers

Byrgyrs cig eidion mêr esgyrn

Beef is a treat and something to savour, so we love to take the time to make a proper burger and enjoy it. There are three things that make this recipe special: mincing the beef just before cooking (but if you need to buy mince it'll still work), adding just the right amount of bone marrow and having all your burger components laid out ready for when the burger comes off the grill. Just before you put the burgers on the grill, season generously. This will help form a crust on the burger and will keep in all those wonderful juices.

800g/1lb 12oz chuck steak

100g/3½oz bone marrow (from about 250g/9oz beef bones cut lengthways)

Flaked sea salt and freshly ground black pepper

Smoked sea salt

To serve

4 brioche burger buns

4 leaves of Little Gem lettuce

4 large slices of tomato

8 large slices of gherkin

4 large slices of onion

4 slices of a good melting cheese, such as Gouda

4 slices of grilled bacon (p.136)

Tomato ketchup or gherkin relish

Mustard

🕐 40 minutes

🍴 4

Preheat a barbecue, if using, or a large cast-iron grill pan.

If you can, mince the meat yourself not too long before you are going to make and cook the burgers. Use the mincing attachment on your mixer (yes, you never thought you'd use it but now is the time) choose the blade with the largest holes. Mince it twice. It's easier to do this when it's fridge cold. If you don't have the equipment, then ask your butcher to do this for you.

Remove the marrow from the bones with a spoon and dice into 1cm/½in cubes. Mix into the minced beef, then form the mixture into four patties by hand or using a burger press. If they are going to be cooked on the barbecue then give them an extra squeeze to ensure they don't break apart. They might seem big but they will shrink a little when cooked. If you make a small indentation on both sides of the burger, it will stop the patty turning into a meatball when being cooked.

Season the burgers heavily just before putting on the hot barbecue or very hot cast-iron grill pan (no oil necessary). Don't squeeze the burger (you've worked so hard to put all the nice fat in there) but do move it around frequently for 4 minutes on each side for a medium-rare burger with a nice crust. Once you have cooked the first side and flipped over, add a slice of cheese to each burger. To aid the melting, add a cloche (or old saucepan) over the top of the burger to keep the heat in, if you like.

When you're about a minute away, add the buns, cut-side down, to the grill and warm the bread throughout. Watch them like a hawk as the sweetness in the bread means they can go from cold to burnt in the blink of an eye.

Remove the buns and burgers from the grill and start building your burger. Spread your sauce of choice over the top bun and set aside. Add mustard on the bottom bun followed by a lettuce leaf, slice of onion and tomato, then add the burger with its safety helmet of cheese, bacon, gherkin and finally, add the ketchup-covered top bun.

French onion soup

We took Margaret, Alison's mother, to Paris for her 89th birthday, as she always wanted to go. The main event was a classically chic lunch of herbed soufflé, cured meats, wine and Provençal olives, but the real star was the starter: a deeply savoury French onion soup that you felt you could disappear into, served with the best baguette croutons we've ever had. We now have a soft spot for this soup, as just one spoonful takes us back to that day. Our version is vegetarian so more people can enjoy it and we use a punchy Dijon mustard, dry sherry and soy sauce for a richer flavour.

2 tbsp salted butter

1 tbsp neutral cooking oil

5 large white onions, finely sliced

2 tsp flaked sea salt

½ tsp soft light brown sugar

6 thyme sprigs

3 bay leaves

175ml/6fl oz dry white wine

1 tbsp Dijon Mustard
  (smoky if you have it)

1.75 litres/3 pints good-quality
  vegetable stock

2 tbsp light soy sauce

1 tbsp black garlic ketchup (optional)

4 tbsp dry sherry
  (such as Manzanilla or Fino)

Freshly ground black pepper

For the croutons

8 slices of baguette, cut at a slight angle

1 garlic clove, peeled

8 tsp Dijon mustard
  (smoky if you have it)

150g/5¼oz Gruyère cheese, grated

🕐 1 hour 15 minutes

🍴 4

Heat the butter and oil in a large saucepan with a lid over a medium heat until the butter starts to sizzle. Add the onions and salt (salting the onions early is crucial for the flavour), cover with the lid and cook, stirring occasionally, for 10 minutes, or until the onions are translucent. Uncover, reduce the heat to low and cook, stirring frequently, for another 10 minutes, or until the onions begin to take on golden edges. Sprinkle over the sugar and a good grind of black pepper, then stir through the onions. Cook for another 25 minutes, or until the onions are deeply caramelised. Taste a slice of onion – it should taste sweet and jammy.

Add the herbs, wine and mustard and stir to combine. Cook for 2–3 minutes until all the wine has been absorbed. Add the stock, soy sauce and ketchup, if using, and stir to combine. Taste the soup and add more salt and/or pepper, if you prefer. Bring to a simmer, then cook, uncovered, for 20 minutes, or until slightly thickened (remember the croutons will absorb a lot of liquid from the soup in the bowls).

When ready to serve, preheat the grill. Lightly toast the baguette slices in a toaster or under the grill, then rub each slice with the garlic clove. Arrange the slices on a baking sheet and spread each slice with some of the mustard. Top with the grated cheese and grill until melted and bubbling.

Divide the sherry between four serving bowls, pour the onion soup on top and add a couple of cheesy croutons to each bowl. The soup can be made up to three days in advance and stored in an airtight container in the fridge until ready to reheat and serve.

Tide pizzas

Pizzas Llanw

During the pandemic, we bought a beautiful wood-fired oven for our outdoor café, Tide/Llanw. The sheer joy it brought people to have a plan to go outside, even if it was only collecting a pizza, for the first time in months, was infectious. Cooking pizza is a great communal activity, but as only one can cook at a time, they are best shared and eaten straight away while the rest cook. We've included two of our favourite topping options here – the first is Sam's recipe (the chef working at the café during lockdown) and the second is an Anna Shepherd special, which is best eaten with a very cold glass of white wine.

For the dough
50ml/1¾fl oz extra virgin olive oil, plus extra for oiling
650g/1lb 7oz strong white bread flour, plus extra for dusting
10g/¼oz fast-action dried yeast
12g/¼oz finer flaked sea salt
450ml/15¼fl oz warm water
Semolina, for dusting

 50–55 minutes, plus 90 minutes rising

Makes 4 large pizzas

The dough

Lightly oil a large bowl and set aside. Put the flour, yeast and salt into another large bowl and stir to combine. Make a well in the centre and pour in the olive oil and warm water, then using clean hands, mix together until combined. Transfer the dough to a clean work surface or a stand mixer fitted with a dough hook attachment. The dough will be sticky and feel more wet than bread dough, so don't be tempted to add more flour at this stage. If you have a dough scraper, use it to help you knead the dough for 10 minutes by stretching the dough away from you and folding it over itself to work more air into the dough as you go, turning 90 degrees after each fold. Alternatively, knead in the mixer for 5–7 minutes until smooth. When the dough 'bounces back' when poked, transfer to the oiled bowl, cover and leave to rise at room temperature for up to 90 minutes, or until doubled in size. Alternatively, you can put it into the fridge for up to 24 hours for a more complex flavour.

Lightly dust a large baking sheet with flour. Tip the risen dough out onto a lightly dusted work surface and cut it into four even-sized pieces, then shape into rounds by pulling the dough from the sides and tucking it underneath, rotating into a round as you go.

Place the shaped dough on the prepared sheet, cover with a clean tea towel and leave to rest in the fridge for up to 12 hours, or until ready to use.

Note
This dough can be made in advance, shaped into rounds, then frozen in a plastic bag up to three months before cooking. Defrost completely at room temperature before stretching and cooking if using from frozen.

Harissa, squash + lemon pizzas

Very thinly sliced lemon on a pizza is a revelation. We have a talented chef called Sam Lomas to thank for that idea.

500g/1lb 2oz butternut or Crown Prince squash, peeled, deseeded and cut into bite-sized chunks

2 tsp flaked sea salt

2 tbsp extra virgin olive oil, plus extra for drizzling

6 red chillies, deseeded (optional)

1 tsp cumin seeds

2 garlic cloves

½ tsp freshly ground black pepper, plus extra to season the squash

1 tbsp tomato purée

1 tsp finer flaked sea salt

Handful of pumpkin seeds

2 unwaxed lemon

Preheat the oven to 200°C/180°C fan/400°F/Gas 6.

Dress the squash with the flaked sea salt, a few grinds of black pepper and a good glug of olive oil. Arrange the squash on a large baking sheet with the chillies. They can share a tray, but don't mix them up; you want the chillies to be dark and crinkly and the squash to be soft and yielding. Roast in the oven for 30 minutes, then remove from the oven and leave to cool slightly.

Blend the cooled squash with a little more olive oil and about 1 tablespoon water to form a loose purée. Separately, blend the roasted chillies with the cumin, garlic, pepper, tomato purée and the finer flaked sea salt. This harissa is excellent on eggs if you have any leftover.

Assemble your pizzas (follow instructions for shaping pizza dough opposite) with a smear of squash, dots of harissa, a handful of pumpkin seeds and a good drizzle of olive oil. Finish with very thinly sliced (best to use a mandolin) lemon, then follow the cooking instructions opposite.

Potato, asparagus + leek pizza bianca

For the caramelised leeks

40g/1½oz butter

4 leeks, finely sliced into 5mm/¼in rounds

1 tsp finer flaked sea salt

½ whole nutmeg

For the pizza topping

250g/9oz buffalo mozzarella

2 new potatoes, very finely sliced on a mandolin and stored in cold water

250g/9oz bunch of asparagus, thick stalks halved lengthways

2 rosemary sprigs, leaves picked

Extra virgin olive oil, for drizzling

Flaked sea salt and freshly ground black pepper

For the caramelised leeks, heat the butter in a large frying pan over a medium heat until melted and sizzling. Add the leeks and salt and cook for 8 minutes, stirring occasionally, until most of the liquid from the leeks has evaporated and they look a brighter shade of green. Reduce the heat to low and cook, stirring occasionally, for 25 minutes, or until the leeks look caramelised in places and taste sweet and jammy. Remove from the heat and grate over the nutmeg.

Dot teaspoons of the leeks over the stretched-out pizza dough and tear over a quarter of the mozzarella. Pat the potato slices dry on kitchen paper, then arrange a few asparagus spears and potato slices over the pizza. Scatter over a quarter of the rosemary leaves, a pinch of flaked salt, a grind of black pepper and drizzle a little olive oil over the top, then follow the cooking instructions opposite.

To cook

If cooking the pizzas in the oven (rather than a dedicated outdoor pizza oven), preheat the oven as high as it will go (at least 240°C/220°C fan/475°F/Gas 9) and place a pizza stone or inverted baking sheet on the middle shelf. Preheat the pizza stone for at least 1 hour before cooking the pizzas.

To shape the pizza dough, place one of the rounds on a lightly floured work surface and use the heel of your hand to push the dough out from the centre to stretch it. Turn the dough slightly with each stretch until the dough forms a rough 22cm/8½in round that is slightly thicker around the edge. Lift onto a flat tray (without a lip), or pizza peel lightly dusted with semolina and shake gently to check that the dough moves over the semolina – this will prevent it sticking as you slide the pizza into the oven to cook.

Slide the pizza onto the preheated baking sheet or pizza stone in the oven. If the oven is hotter than 240°C/220°C fan/475°F/ Gas 9, reduce the heat to 240°C/220°C fan/475°F/Gas 9 and cook for 9–11 minutes until the edges are puffed up and crispy and the cheese is golden and bubbling. Slice into wedges and serve, one pizza at a time to share, while you cook the remaining pizzas.

Chicken Caesar salad

Salad Cesar cyw iâr

For the brine

1 litre/35fl oz tap water

100g/3½oz muscovado sugar

150g/5¼oz finer flaked sea salt

6 juniper berries

6 cloves

1 star anise

6 black peppercorns

2 bay leaves, shredded

For the chicken

1 medium free-range chicken, jointed

Finely grated zest and juice of 1 lemon

6 garlic cloves, grated

Handful of parsley, leaves chopped

3 tbsp olive oil

Salt and freshly ground black pepper

For the croutons

100ml/3½fl oz olive oil, plus extra if needed

4 slices of stale sourdough bread, torn into bite-sized chunks, or if really stale, sliced into thin slivers (2 handfuls)

For the dressing

1 medium egg yolk

6 anchovy fillets in oil

1 tbsp white wine vinegar

1 tsp Dijon mustard

1 garlic clove, crushed

30g/1oz Parmesan cheese, finely grated

2 tbsp sunflower oil

4 tbsp natural yogurt

Juice of ½ lemon

Salt and freshly ground black pepper

For the salad bits

2 Romaine or 4 Little Gem lettuces

6 pickled anchovy fillets, sliced lengthways

Handful of large Parmesan cheese shavings

4 soft-boiled eggs, quartered

The reputation of this salad has been sullied over the years, thanks to limp leaves in plastic containers, found lurking in the chillers of service stations. Rest assured that we're about to put that right. It's the layering of flavours that really makes this classic dish a winner – succulent chicken, crispy salty skin, garlic marinade, anchovies and Parmesan for added umami.

Put all the brine ingredients into a large saucepan and heat until the salt and sugar have dissolved. Remove from the heat and leave the brine to cool.

Put the cooled brine and chicken pieces into a large non-reactive food container, cover and store overnight in the fridge. The brine will ensure the chicken remains moist during cooking.

The next day, preheat the grill to high.

Wash the brine off the chicken and pat dry. Season the chicken all over with salt and pepper and place in a large roasting tray, skin side up, under the grill. You can also do this on the hob in a very hot heavy grill pan, searing the chicken skin-side down. Once the chicken skin has crisped, remove from the grill and preheat the oven to 160°C/140°C fan/325°F/Gas 3.

Mix the lemon zest and juice, garlic, parsley and olive oil together in a large bowl, season to taste, then pour over the chicken pieces, making sure everything is well coated in the mixture. Place the chicken in the oven, skin-side up, for 30 minutes, or until the juices run clear when a skewer is inserted into the thickest part of the meat.

Once the chicken is cooked, remove from the roasting tray and leave to rest on a board or plate but keep the oven on. Retain the chicken juices and garlic-infused oil in the tray. You may need to loosen the juices with a little more olive oil. Toss the bread for the croutons in the tray until completely coated, then roast in the oven for 15 minutes, or until crispy.

To make the dressing, put all ingredients, except the sunflower oil, yogurt and lemon juice, into a blender and blend until smooth, then start dribbling in the oil. Once all the oil has been mixed through, stir in the yogurt and season with salt, pepper and lemon juice.

To a large serving platter, add the lettuce leaves and dress with half of the dressing, then add the chicken, croutons, anchovies, Parmesan and eggs. Dot the remaining dressing over the salad and serve.

Salt + pepper smoked ribs

Asennau mŵg halen a phupur

Sometimes it's the simple things that work the best. In this recipe the combination of sea salt, pepper and smoke provide all the flavour you need. The only other key element is time. Lots of it. Thankfully it's time that can be spent while also having a drink and talking to friends. You will need a barbecue that allows you to cook on indirect heat and keep the smoke in. Given that smoke will be a key ingredient in your dish, make sure you cook with good-quality charcoal and wood. The other essential bit of kit is a thermometer. Set this up to measure the temperature in the dome of the barbecue.

3–4 handfuls of apple or cherry wood
    chips or chunks, for smoking
4 racks of baby back ribs
2–3 tbsp sunflower or groundnut oil
25g/1oz finer flaked sea salt
25g/1oz freshly ground black pepper
50:50 blend of apple cider vinegar
    and apple juice, for spritzing – about
    500ml/18fl oz in total (optional)

🕐 6 hours

🍴 2 as a main, or 4 as a side

Preheat a barbecue for indirect cooking with glowing coals set to the side of the grill or under the heat shields. Add a few chips of your favourite smoking wood and adjust the airflow to achieve an air temperature in the kettle of 100–130°C/210–260°F. You should see small wisps of white/almost blue smoke escaping from the air vents. If this upgrades to white billowy smoke, then there is too much air going into the barbecue.

To prepare the meat, either remove the membrane from the underside of the ribs or ask your butcher to do this for you. Oil the ribs with a tiny amount of oil, liberally season with the salt and pepper and set on the grill for 3 hours. Adjust the barbecue to try and keep the temperature in the target range. Try to resist opening too many times but if you do, and you want to feel like a real pitmaster, spray the ribs with a 50:50 mix of apple cider vinegar and apple juice. This helps form a 'bark' on the ribs and, along with the salt, helps the smoke flavour to stick to the meat.

When the ribs are cooked, remove from the grill and put on to a double layer of foil. Tightly wrap the ribs in the foil being careful not to rip the foil on any protruding bones, then return the foil parcel to the grill for another 2 hours. This stage of the cook ensures that 'falling-off-the-bone' final product.

Carefully remove the ribs from the grill and open the foil pocket over a baking dish to catch all the cooking juices. The final stage of the cook is to 'set' the ribs. Return the ribs to the grill for a final hour, coating the ribs with the cooking juices every 10–15 minutes until the time is up and you can't wait any longer.

Serve with cold beer, pickles and napkins.

Anglesey salt + pepper fritto misto

Fritto misto halen a phupur Ynys Môn

This is holiday food. The best fritto misto we can remember was in Italy – sugar paper cones filled with an array of tender green veg and seafood, sprinkled with coarse sea salt and washed down with very cold beers. Depending on the season, you can mix up the veg according to your favourites – we like asparagus in late spring/early summer; courgettes in late summer; finely sliced sweet squashes in autumn; and trimmed purple sprouting broccoli in winter. We like to serve this with our Garlic Mayonnaise on p.38.

10g/¼oz dried seaweed,
  such as kombu or dulse
200g/7oz courgettes,
  cut into 1cm/½in rounds
50g/1¾oz curly kale, leaves torn into
  bite-sized pieces
100g/3½oz green beans or asparagus
  spears, cut into bite-sized pieces
400g/14oz prepared mixed seafood, such
  as squid, cleaned and cut into rings;
  prawns, peeled and heads removed;
  flaky white fish, such as MSC cod,
  plaice or haddock, filleted and cut into
  3cm/1¼in chunks
1 litre/35fl oz vegetable oil,
  for deep-frying
150g/5¼oz plain flour
1 tbsp cornflour
75g/2¾oz fine semolina
1 tsp baking powder
½ tsp finer flaked sea salt
½ tsp coarsely ground black pepper,
  plus extra for sprinkling
2 medium egg whites
300ml/10½fl oz sparkling water
Flaked sea salt
1 lemon, cut into wedges, to serve

 35–45 minutes

 6 as a starter

Put the seaweed into a small bowl, cover with water and leave to soak for 5 minutes, then drain and set aside. Pat all the vegetables and seafood dry between two clean tea towels.

Preheat the oven to 120°C/100°C fan/250°F/Gas 1. Line a large baking sheet with kitchen paper and sit a wire rack on top of it to drain the cooked pieces.

Pour the oil for deep-frying into a large saucepan, so that it comes 4cm/1½in up the sides. Clip a sugar thermometer to the side of the pan and heat the oil over a medium-high heat.

Meanwhile, mix both flours, the semolina, baking powder, salt and pepper together in a large bowl. Whisk the egg whites in another bowl until thick, bright white and frothy but before they start to form soft peaks. Set aside.

Pour the sparkling water into the flour mixture and whisk to combine, then fold through the whisked egg whites until the mixture is smooth.

When the oil reaches 180°C/350°F on the thermometer, drop a handful of fish, vegetables and seaweed into the batter, allowing any excess batter to drip back into the bowl. Carefully lower the coated pieces into the hot oil immediately, using a clean slotted spoon to separate the pieces to prevent clumping. Deep-fry for 4–5 minutes, turning the pieces once until crisp and golden on both sides. Lift the pieces with the slotted spoon onto the prepared wire rack and immediately sprinkle with flaked sea salt.

Allow the oil to come back up to temperature before repeating with the remaining vegetables, fish and batter, transferring the batches to the wire rack to drain as you go and seasoning with salt while they are hot. Keep the cooked pieces warm in the oven with the door slightly ajar while you cook the rest (this will prevent the batter going soggy).

Serve on a platter with the lemon wedges. Grind over some more black pepper and eat with friends and plenty of paper napkins.

Perfect garlic mushrooms

Madarch garlleg hyfryd

This recipe works for more exotic mushroom lovers among us (Hamish) as well as people like me (Alison) who are not so mushroom-curious and prefer to stick to the straight-up button type. Once the mushrooms are in the pan, everything happens quite quickly so it helps to have all your ingredients prepared beforehand. If you don't have dry sherry, use the same amount of dry white wine instead. These mushrooms are delicious with Dijon mustard either served on the side, or stirred through at the end.

500g/1lb 2oz mixed or button mushrooms, cleaned and torn into roughly even-sized pieces
2 tsp finer flaked sea salt
40g/1½oz butter
4 garlic cloves, crushed
50ml/1¾fl oz dry sherry, such as Fino or Mazanilla
4 tbsp full-fat crème fraîche
½ small bunch of tarragon, chopped
½ small bunch of parsley, chopped
Freshly ground black pepper
4 slices of hot buttered toast, to serve

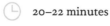 20–22 minutes

 4

Heat a large non-stick frying pan over a high heat, add the mushrooms, then scatter 1½ teaspoons of the salt over them and cook, stirring frequently, for 5 minutes, or until the mushrooms have reduced in volume by two-thirds and are catching and turning golden in places. Reduce the heat to medium, push the mushrooms to one side of the pan and add the butter to the empty space. Cook for another 3 minutes, stirring to coat the mushrooms in the melted butter. Add the garlic and cook, stirring constantly, for 90 seconds, or until the garlic smells intensely fragrant.

Reduce the heat to low and pour in the sherry. Cook for 1 minute until most of the liquid has been absorbed, then remove from the heat and stir in the crème fraîche and herbs. Season well with black pepper.

Spoon the mushrooms over slices of toast and serve immediately with the remaining salt on the side for sprinkling.

Parsnip + Cheddar croquettes

Croquettes pannas a Cheddar

Crisp, seasoned breadcrumbs give way to a delicately balanced, pillowy interior in these excellent little croquettes. We've used untraditional parsnips for a deeper flavour, but the characteristic crunch of the croquette remains, as well as the final flourish of flaked sea salt, which is essential. We serve these with fried eggs, Marcona almonds, rich tomato stews, or with a little mayonnaise (p.38) and a spoon of Spiced Tomato Chutney (p.106).

500g/1lb 2oz parsnips, peeled and cut
  into 4cm/1½in pieces
500g/1lb 2oz floury potatoes
  (such as King Edward or Maris Piper),
  peeled and cut into 4cm/1½in pieces
1 bunch of spring onions, white and light
  green parts finely sliced
¼ tsp dried chilli flakes
115g/4oz strong hard cheese,
  such as Cheddar or Gruyère, grated
1 heaped tsp wholegrain mustard
25g/1oz butter, melted
4 medium eggs
75g/2¾oz plain flour
100g/3½oz panko breadcrumbs
Vegetable oil, for deep-frying
1 lemon, cut into wedges
Finer flaked sea salt and freshly ground
  black pepper
Flaked sea salt, to finish
Mace Mayonnaise (p.38),
  to serve

Note
You can bake the croquettes
instead of deep-frying them,
although the fried version is
infinitely better. Preheat the oven
to 220°C/200°C fan/425°F/Gas 7.
Drizzle the croquettes with olive oil
and bake in the oven for about
20–25 minutes until piping
hot and golden.

Put the parsnips and potatoes into a large saucepan and cover with
cold water. Add 1 tablespoon of finer flaked salt and bring to the boil.
Boil for 15 minutes, or until the parsnips and potatoes are tender
throughout. Drain in a colander and leave to steam-dry for 15 minutes,
then put into a large bowl and mash until smooth. Stir in the spring
onions, chilli flakes, cheese, mustard and melted butter, then season
with ½ teaspoon finer flaked salt and a generous grind of black pepper.
Taste the mixture and add more salt if you prefer. When you are
happy with the seasoning, mix through one of the eggs to combine.

Beat the remaining eggs in a wide, shallow bowl. Spread the flour out
on a large plate and season lightly with salt and pepper. Spread the
breadcrumbs out on a separate plate. Line a couple of baking sheets
with baking paper.

Using clean (or gloved) hands, divide the mixture into rough
45g/1½oz balls, then shape into croquette cylinder shapes. Roll in
the flour, then dip into the egg to coat and finally roll through the
breadcrumbs until they are covered all over. Put the coated croquettes
on to the prepared baking sheet as you go. When you have shaped all
the croquettes, chill in the fridge for 20 minutes to firm up.

Pour the vegetable oil for deep-frying into a large saucepan, so it
comes 5cm/2in up the sides of the pan. Clip a sugar thermometer
onto the side of the pan and heat the oil over a medium-high heat.
Line another baking sheet with kitchen paper and preheat the oven to
120°C/100°C fan/250°F/Gas 1.

When the oil reaches 180°C/350°F on the thermometer, carefully
lower the croquettes, in batches, into the hot oil and deep-fry for
2–3 minutes until crisp on the underside. Use a slotted spoon to gently
flip them over and cook for another 2–3 minutes. Remove with a
slotted spoon and leave to drain on the lined baking sheet, then keep
warm in the oven with the door slightly ajar (this will prevent the
croquettes losing their distinctive crunchy exterior). Repeat with the
remaining, uncooked croquettes. They will keep warm for 1 hour
before overcooking.

When ready to serve, arrange on a platter with lemon wedges for
squeezing over. Scatter over a generous pinch of flaked salt and serve
with the mayonnaise.

Welsh mussels + chips

1 hour, plus
30–60 minutes soaking

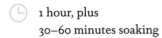

4

As well as being absolutely delicious, mussels have the added bonus of being very sustainable, as growing them requires almost no input as they don't require feeding or fertiliser to grow, unlike salmon for example. The clean seas around the isle of Anglesey not only mean that we produce amazing sea salt here, but we can also grow incredible mussels and oysters. This recipe celebrates the humble mussel, with the addition of Welsh leeks and the very best oven chips you can make at home.

For the mussels
2kg/4lb 6½oz live mussels

50g/1¾oz butter

2 tbsp extra virgin olive oil

3 leeks, finely sliced into rounds

4 celery sticks, finely chopped

6 garlic cloves, finely sliced

2 fresh bay leaves

250ml/8¾ fl oz dry Welsh cider

Small bunch of parsley, leaves picked
    and roughly chopped

Small bunch of tarragon, leaves picked
    and roughly chopped

Flaked sea salt and freshly ground
    black pepper

For the chips
1.5kg/3lb 4¾oz floury potatoes
    (such as King Edward or Maris Piper)

Vegetable oil, for roasting

Mayonnaise (p.38), to serve

Put the mussels into a large bowl of cold water, making sure they are submerged. Place a colander in the sink nearby. Tap any open mussels on a hard surface (such as the side of the sink) to ensure they close before transferring to the colander. Discard any mussels that remain open after tapping as it's an indication that they are dead. As you go, scrub the mussels and remove their beards. Suspend the colander over a clean bowl and transfer to the fridge until you are ready to cook them.

Cut the potatoes into chips, sized somewhere between a French fry and a chip shop chip. Lower all of the prepared chips into a large bowl filled with cold water, making sure that the surface of the water completely covers the potatoes and leave to soak for about 30–60 minutes. This will help to draw out the starch from the potatoes, ensuring they crisp up as they cook.

Preheat the oven to 220°C/200°C fan/425°F/Gas 7.

Drain the potatoes in a colander, then thoroughly pat dry. Pour enough vegetable oil into two large roasting trays so that the oil completely covers the base by at least 2mm/¹⁄₁₆in. Transfer the trays to the oven for 3 minutes to heat the oil, then one at a time, remove the trays from the oven, and very carefully divide the dried potatoes onto each tray. Use a spatula to turn the potatoes over in the hot oil so that every side is coated. Roast the chips in the oven for 40–50 minutes, opening the oven door every 10 minutes to release the steam and jiggle the potatoes around to prevent them sticking. If one shelf in your oven is hotter, swap the trays around so they cook evenly.

Twenty minutes before the end of the chip cooking time, heat the butter and olive oil in a deep saucepan over a medium heat until the butter is melted and bubbling. Add the leeks, celery, a pinch of salt and a generous grind of black pepper and cook, stirring frequently for 10 minutes, or until the vegetables are soft and translucent, but not yet caramelising at the edges. Stir in the garlic and bay leaves and cook for 1–2 minutes until fragrant. Add the mussels, cider and all but a handful of the chopped herbs and cover the pan tightly with a lid. Increase the heat to medium-high and cook for 5–7 minutes until all the shells have opened. If there are any mussels that are still tightly shut, discard as it's likely that they are dead and shouldn't be eaten.

Remove the chips from the oven. Lay a long sheet of kitchen paper in the base of a large bowl, so that it hangs over the sides of the bowl. Use a slotted spatula to lift the chips from the tray onto the kitchen paper, then lift the paper away from the bowl, leaving the chips inside. Sprinkle the chips with flaked sea salt and black pepper and toss to coat.

Serve the mussels in warmed bowls with a ladle of the broth poured over and the remaining herbs scattered over the top. Serve the chips separately to keep them crisp. We like to serve mussels and chips with mayonnaise, but they are delicious without, too.

Sherry-braised fennel + almond lasagne

Lasagne ffenigl drwy sieri ac almwnd

 2 hours 5 minutes

 6

Let's face it, lasagne does take a little time and care to prepare, but this one, we promise, is worth it. Much of the seasoning comes from the already salty ingredients – the Parmesan and capers. It's a celebration of grown-up flavours with a real depth from the sherry and all the green vegetables.

125g/4½oz butter,
   plus extra for greasing
2 fennel bulbs, finely sliced
2 leeks, finely sliced
2 celery sticks, finely sliced
1 onion, finely sliced
3¼ tsp finer flaked sea salt
3 bay leaves
100g/3½oz curly kale or cavolo nero
5 tbsp capers in brine,
   drained and rinsed
150ml/5fl oz dry sherry,
   such as Fino or Manzanilla
2 garlic cloves, finely chopped
100g/3½oz almonds, toasted
   and roughly chopped
75g/2¾oz plain flour
650ml/22fl oz whole milk
200ml/7 fl oz vegetable stock
100g/3½oz Parmesan cheese,
   finely grated
¼ whole nutmeg, grated
250g/9oz mascarpone cheese
1 medium egg, beaten
Small bunch of parsley, finely chopped
12 sheets of dried lasagne
4 oregano sprigs, leaves picked
   (optional)
Freshly ground black pepper

Melt 50g/1¾oz of the butter in a large sauté pan over a high heat. Add the fennel, leeks, celery, onion and 2 teaspoons of the salt and fry, stirring frequently, for 10 minutes, or until the vegetables have softened and reduced in volume by a third. Reduce the heat to medium-low, stir in the bay leaves and a good grind of black pepper and cook for 30 minutes, stirring occasionally, until all the liquid has evaporated and the vegetables are beginning to catch ever so slightly in places.

Meanwhile, pulse the kale and capers together in a food processor until very finely chopped. Alternatively, finely chop by hand. Set aside.

Pour the sherry into the pan and stir for 30 seconds, or until all the sherry has been absorbed. Add the kale mixture and garlic and stir until the kale is vibrant green and the garlic smells fragrant. Remove from the heat and stir in the almonds.

Preheat the oven to 180°C/160°C fan/350°F/Gas 4. Grease a 20 x 30cm/8 x 12in baking dish with butter.

To make the white sauce for the lasagne, melt the remaining 75g/2¾oz butter in another pan over a medium heat until foaming. Add the flour and stir for 2 minutes, or until the mixture has turned a shade or two darker. Slowly pour in the milk, stirring constantly, then add the stock. Use a whisk to mix the flour and liquid together until combined, then cook without letting the liquid come to the boil, stirring occasionally, for 8–10 minutes until the sauce has thickened and coats the back of a wooden spoon.

Remove from the heat and stir in 40g/1½oz of the Parmesan, 1 teaspoon of the salt and the nutmeg. Set aside.

Beat the mascarpone, all but a handful of the remaining Parmesan (reserve the handful to top the lasagne), the egg, parsley and the remaining ¼ teaspoon of the salt together in a large bowl. Add a good grind of black pepper, too.

Spread a third of the vegetable mixture over the base of the prepared baking dish, top with four of the lasagne sheets, breaking them up if needed to cover the vegetables and meet the sides of the dish. Drizzle a third of the mascarpone mixture over the pasta, followed by the white sauce. Repeat with the remaining vegetables, lasagne sheets and after the final layer of herby mascarpone, cover with the remaining white sauce, using a spatula to spread it to meet the edges of the dish. Scatter over the reserved Parmesan and the oregano leaves, if using. Bake in the oven for 40 minutes, or until the top is bubbling and golden. Cover the lasagne with foil after 30 minutes if it looks as though it might burn.

Serve with a crisp green salad, dressed with Dijon mustard, olive oil, lemon and salt.

Slow-roast hogget shoulder

Ysgwydd cig hesbwrn wedi'i rostio'n araf

 5 hours

 4–6

Very occasionally we get some cold and damp autumn days in Wales, but the weather can't get in the way of life and we truly believe that the harshest elements can be softened by a hearty meal. Hogget is a more mature version of lamb. Those additional days munching grass (lamb less than 12 months, hogget 12–24 months, mutton more than 24 months) transform the sweet lamb into a darker, richer meat, which lends itself to slower cooking. Lamb will work as a substitute if you can't get hold of hogget, although it won't have the depth of flavour that more mature meat does.

25g/1oz butter, softened

2 white onions, sliced

3 large parsnips, finely sliced lengthways

1 small celeriac, peeled and finely sliced

6 garlic cloves, half cut into thin slices, half cut into shards

2 thyme sprigs, leaves picked

2 rosemary sprigs, leaves picked

2 large waxy potatoes (eg. Charlotte or Anya), finely sliced

1 Welsh organic hogget shoulder, about 1.5-2kg/3lb 4¾oz-6lb 6½oz (choose the size according to the appetite of your guests)

500ml/18fl oz vegetable stock

Flaked sea salt and freshly ground black pepper

For the salsa

2 tbsp olive oil

2 tbsp apple cider vinegar

1 garlic clove, crushed or grated

2 Granny Smith apples, cored and cut into matchsticks

1 shallot, finely chopped

Small bunch of mint, leaves picked and finely sliced

1 red chilli, finely chopped, deseeded for a mellow heat

Preheat the oven to 140°C/120°C fan/275°F/Gas 1. Grease a large roasting dish, about 37cm x 25cm/14½ x 10in with half the butter. A heavy cast-iron dish is best but other roasting pans will also work.

Mix the onions, parsnips, celeriac, ½ teaspoon salt, ½ teaspoon pepper, the sliced garlic and half the thyme and rosemary red roasting dish. Add a neat layer of potatoes and a few spots of the remaining butter, then season the top of the potatoes and sprinkle on the remaining thyme.

Pierce the hogget joint with a sharp knife about ten times all over. In each incision, poke in a shard of garlic and a few rosemary leaves. Season all over and place on top of the bed of vegetables.

Warm the stock in a large saucepan until it comes to the boil and pour carefully over the vegetables. Cover the roasting pan tightly with two layers of foil and cook in the oven for 4 hours. (Now is a good time to go and enjoy the weather...)

Remove the foil, increase the oven temperature to 180°C/160°C fan/350°F/Gas 4 and cook for another 30 minutes. This final stage of cooking will crisp up the potatoes and hogget.

To make the apple and mint salsa, mix the olive oil, vinegar and garlic together in a small bowl until thoroughly combined. Add the apples, shallot, mint and chilli and mix just before serving. Season to taste.

Serve the hogget with the salsa and green beans or braised red cabbage.

Four season white bean + greens soup

Cawl ffa gwyn a llysiau gwyrdd y pedwar tymor

25g/1oz butter

6 shallots, finely chopped

1 carrot, finely chopped

1 celery stick, finely chopped

½ tsp finer flaked sea salt, plus extra
  if needed

4 garlic cloves, finely sliced

½ tsp fennel seeds

100g/3½oz frozen peas

600g/1lb 5oz jar white beans,
  such as cannellini or butter beans,
  drained and rinsed

1 litre/35fl oz vegetable stock

50g/1¾oz Parmesan cheese,
  finely grated

Olive oil, for drizzling

Freshly ground black pepper

For the salsa

Small bunch of parsley, leaves picked

1 garlic clove, peeled

1 unwaxed lemon

Spring

200g/7oz spring greens,
  stalks discarded, leaves very finely sliced

Summer

150g/5¼oz spinach and 150g/5¼oz
  cherry tomatoes, halved

Autumn

200g/7oz mature spinach, or rainbow
  chard, stalks very fine sliced, leaves
  stacked and cut into 1cm/½in slices

Winter

200g/7oz cavolo nero, stalks discarded
  and leaves roughly torn

45 minutes

4–6

This is one of our very favourite soup recipes, which is high praise indeed coming from Alison, whose last meal on earth would probably be a bowl of soup. The simple savoury base can be added to according to the seasons, so we make it all year round. Although the ingredients are classic and straightforward, there is a real depth of flavour from the gremolata, which gives a fresh, garlicky hit on top the creamy beans. It is well worth seeking out beans in a jar rather than the tinned variety if you can. Eat this for supper with sourdough and Very Good Homemade Butter (p.43), or toast rubbed with garlic and drizzled with olive oil.

Melt the butter in a large saucepan over a medium heat until melted and sizzling. Add the shallots, carrot and celery, a good grind of black pepper and the salt and fry, stirring occasionally, for 10–12 minutes until everything is completely soft, glossy and fragrant.

Stir in the garlic and fennel seeds and cook for another minute until the anise aroma fills the kitchen. Add the peas and stir to combine, then add the beans and stock and bring to the boil. Reduce the heat to a simmer and taste the soup. The saltiness will depend partly on the generosity of seasoning in the bean jar – add a little more salt, if you prefer. Add the seasonal greens (and tomatoes if making the summer version of the soup) and simmer for 10 minutes, or until the greens are bright green and tender.

Meanwhile, to make the gremolata, finely chop the parsley, lifting any larger leaves up and over the top of the pile as you go, until the leaves on the chopping board are a darker shade of green and very finely chopped. Save the stalks for stock, or to blitz into a pasta sauce. Use a fine grater or Microplane to grate the garlic and lemon zest over the parsley. Chop the garlic and lemon into the parsley to combine, then transfer everything on the board to a bowl.

Ladle the soup into warmed bowls and place 1 teaspoon of the gremolata on top. Scatter over the Parmesan, drizzle with olive oil and serve with lemon wedges for squeezing over.

Well-salted snacks

When we have time, beginning a meal by sharing a generous bowl of salted snacks is often the best part, and these should provide an excellent grazing platter and an alternative to potato crisps to accompany drinks for about 4–6 people. You can swap the spices around with your favourite combinations, if you like. Ground spices can be added to the seeds, dried chilli flakes can be sprinkled on the kale and lemon zest can be grated over all of them.

Spiced seeds

12–14 minutes

200g/7oz mixed seeds (such as pumpkin, sunflower, sesame, linseed)
1 tsp fennel seeds
1 tsp cumin seeds
2 tsp extra virgin olive oil
½ tsp finer flaked sea salt

Preheat the oven to 180°C/160°C fan/350°F/Gas 4. Line a 20 x 30cm/8 x 12in baking sheet with baking paper.

Toss all the seeds and spices together in a small bowl until combined. Add the olive oil and salt and stir until the seeds are coated. Spread the seeds out on the lined baking sheet and bake in the oven for 7–9 minutes until golden. Check the seeds after 5 minutes and shake the sheet, ensuring the seeds don't catch and burn in places.

Serve warm or cool. Store in an airtight container for up to a week. Any leftover seeds can be sprinkled over salads, roasted vegetables or soups for crunch.

Root vegetable crisps

40 minutes, plus 30 minutes cooling

Depending on your skill with the peeler and water content of your vegetables, mixed vegetables will turn crisp at different rates, so some will have tender centres while others have dark, very crisp edges. We like this contrast, but if you prefer things more uniform, just cook one type of vegetable for completely even crispness.

400g/14oz mixed root vegetables, such as parsnips, beetroot, carrots, celeriac, turnips or swede, scrubbed well and tops removed (prepared weight)
2 tbsp extra virgin olive oil
Flaked sea salt, for sprinkling

Preheat the oven to 150°C/130°C fan/300°F/Gas 2.

Using a speed peeler, peel the vegetables into long, thin ribbons over a large bowl. When your fingertips are in danger of being peeled too, move onto the next vegetable. Keep the centre of the peeled root for stock.

Pour the olive oil over the vegetables and, using clean hands, mix well until every ribbon is coated in oil. Spread the vegetables out in a single, even layer on two large baking sheets and bake in the oven for 35–40 minutes, opening the door every 10 minutes to release the steam and stirring twice during this time. Move the sheets around a couple of times if your oven is hotter in one place.

When the vegetables are brown in places and mostly crisp, transfer to a wire rack to cool completely and crisp up for 30 minutes, then toss with a generous pinch of flaked salt. Store in an airtight container for up to 24 hours until ready to serve.

Crispy kale

100g/3½oz curly kale, stalks removed and
   torn into bite-sized pieces (prepared weight)
2 tbsp extra virgin olive oil
1 tsp Halen Môn pure sea salt with chilli
   and garlic (or other sea salt flavour of
   your choice)

Preheat the oven to 120°C/100°C fan/250°F/Gas ½.

Put all the ingredients into a large bowl, and using clean hands, rub together until the kale is glossy and each piece is dressed lightly in oil.

Spread the kale out in a single, even layer on a large baking sheet and bake for 30 minutes, opening the door every 10 minutes to release the steam – this will help the kale crisp up. Remove from the oven and serve immediately, or store in an airtight container for up to 24 hours after the kale has cooled completely.

Crispy fried sage leaves

20 minutes

If you've not had these before, why not? Sage is the star here, so look for perky leaves. It's important to have cold fizzy water as the greater the difference in temperature between the water and the oil, the more the batter will react with the hot oil as it cooks, turning the battered sage leaves extra crisp and light. Make the batter up to 1 hour in advance and keep covered in the fridge until ready to use. The batter will make more than you need, but can be used to batter small fish like sardines, anchovies and sprats for whitebait. Alternatively, try dipping edible flowers and delicate leaves such as courgette flowers or tender baby beetroot leaves in the batter to serve alongside.

60g/2¼oz plain flour
40g/1½oz rice flour
1 medium egg, beaten
220ml/7½fl oz cold sparkling water
500ml/18fl oz vegetable oil, for deep-frying
50 sage leaves, rinsed and dried
Finer flaked sea salt, to finish

Mix the flours together in a medium bowl. Make a well in the centre and add the egg. Pour in the cold sparkling water and use a whisk to mix until the mixture is smooth and it resembles pancake batter.

Line a plate with kitchen paper and place near the hob. Pour the vegetable oil into a large saucepan, clip a sugar thermometer on to the side and heat over a medium-high heat. When the temperature reaches 190°C/375°F on the thermometer, dip the sage leaves into the batter in batches of 10, then carefully lower into the hot oil. Deep-fry for 45–60 seconds until they are golden brown around the edges. Remove the leaves with a slotted spoon and drain on the lined plate, shaking any excess oil off over the pan.

Scatter a pinch of salt over the cooked sage leaves and repeat with the remaining leaves and batter. Serve immediately.

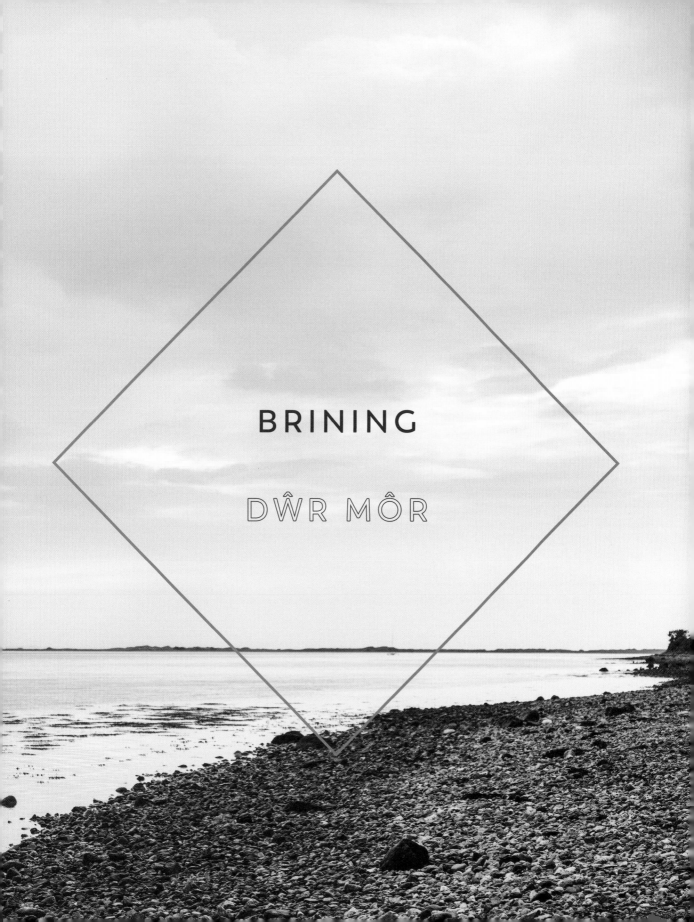

BRINING

DŴR MÔR

Caramelised leek + thyme focaccia

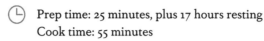

Focaccia cennin wedi'i garameleiddio a theim

Our focaccia takes on more of a Welsh flavour than an Italian one, with the addition of perfectly caramelised leeks and the scent of thyme. The method here, using a brine, is a technique we have borrowed from the ever brilliant American chef and author, Samin Nosrat, as it gives the bread a wonderful crispy top and a generous rise. This recipe uses the whole leek, so don't discard the tops. They tend to hold their shape better than the creamier white base of the leek, making for a lovely contrast of textures.

For the dough

650ml/22fl oz lukewarm water

¾ tsp fast-action dried yeast

1 tbsp caster sugar

775g/1lb 11oz strong white bread flour

1½ tbsp finer flaked sea salt

60ml/2fl oz extra virgin olive oil, plus extra for drizzling

2 tbsp butter, for greasing

3 thyme sprigs, leaves picked

½ tsp flaked sea salt

Freshly ground black pepper

For the brine

75ml/2½fl oz lukewarm water

1½ tsp finer flaked sea salt

For the leeks

1 tbsp extra virgin olive oil

3 leeks (about 350g/12¼oz), sliced into 1cm/½in rounds

½ tsp finer flaked sea salt

⅛ whole nutmeg, grated

Prep time: 25 minutes, plus 17 hours resting
Cook time: 55 minutes

8

Start by preparing the dough. Mix the water, yeast and sugar together in a large jug until the yeast has dissolved, then leave for about 10 minutes, or until the mixture is bubbly. Mix the flour and salt together in a large bowl to combine. Make a well in the centre and pour in the yeast mixture and oil. Use a spatula to mix everything together until the dough is uniform and no dry patches are visible. Cover the bowl with a clean, dry tea towel and leave at room temperature overnight or for 14–16 hours until the dough has doubled in size and small holes are visible on the surface.

The next day, grease the base and sides of a 26 x 36cm/10½ x 14in baking dish with the butter. Prepare the brine by mixing the water and salt together in a bowl until the salt dissolves. Pour the dough into the centre of the greased dish and use clean hands to stretch the dough into all four corners. It's a slightly sticky job as the dough is much wetter than a standard loaf. When the dough is stretched, use your fingers to poke dimples all over the surface and pour over a generous glug (about 2 tablespoons) of the oil. Pour the brine over the surface too. Cover and leave to prove at room temperature for another hour.

Preheat the oven to 220°C/200°C fan/425°F/Gas 7 and place a pizza stone or baking sheet on the middle shelf to heat up.

Meanwhile, make a start on the leeks. Heat the oil in a large frying pan over a medium-high heat for a minute. Add the leeks and the salt and fry, stirring occasionally, for 8 minutes until the leeks are completely soft, vibrant and there is almost no liquid left in the pan, taking care not to let the leeks take on too much colour as they cook. Reduce the heat to low and cook for another 8 minutes, or until the leeks are beginning to turn golden in places and are completely soft. Remove from the heat and grate over the nutmeg.

Dimple the focaccia dough again with clean fingers and use a spoon to dot the cooked leeks over the top. Scatter the thyme leaves over the surface of the dough, then finish with a generous grind of black pepper and the flaked salt over the top.

Bake in the centre of the oven for 20 minutes, or until risen. Check the focaccia after this time; if the leeks look as though they are beginning to catch and burn, cover with foil and pierce all over with a sharp knife to allow the steam to escape and the bread to crisp up. Cook for another 15–18 minutes until deep golden and crisp on the surface. Tap the base of the pan to check that it sounds hollow – this is a sign that the bread is airy and cooked through. Remove from the heat and drizzle or brush with a generous glug of olive oil (about 2 tablespoons). The surface will look oily, but the bread will absorb the oil as it cools. Leave the focaccia to cool in the tin for 10 minutes before using two sturdy cake slices or spatulas to release all four edges and lift onto a wire rack.

Eat warm or at room temperature. The focaccia is best eaten the day it is cooked, but can be frozen in a sealed bag, wrapped in baking paper, or stored like this at room temperature and gently reheated in a hot oven for 8 minutes to refresh.

Herb-brined lemon sole with green beans + almonds

Lleden lyfn drwy heli perlysiau gyda ffa gwyrdd ac almwndau

For the brined fish

500ml/18fl oz freshly boiled water

25g/1oz finer flaked sea salt

4 lemon sole fillets

2 celery sticks, leaves picked and stalks
cut into 3cm/1¼in pieces

1 lemon, peel pared (save the fruit to
serve alongside the fish in wedges)

3 thyme sprigs

3 parsley stalks

3 dill stalks or fennel fronds

5 black peppercorns

50g/1¾oz plain flour

Butter and olive oil, for frying

Freshly ground black pepper

Lemon wedges, to serve

For the beans

1 round shallot or ½ banana shallot,
finely chopped

2 tbsp sherry vinegar

1½ tsp caster sugar

250g/9oz fine beans, trimmed

75g/2¾oz butter

50g/1¾oz almonds, toasted
and roughly chopped

½ bunch of parsley, leaves only,
finely chopped

Finer flaked sea salt and freshly ground
black pepper

Prep time: 25 minutes, plus 15 minutes brining
Cook time: 25 minutes.

4

This is one of those amazing dishes that looks and tastes like something you might order in a restaurant, but is actually simple to make. Brining fish quickly before cooking seasons it all the way through. It also helps to firm up the muscle fibres, making it easier to fry without falling apart, as well as preventing it from drying out during cooking. Feel free to switch up the aromatics used in the brine, but the recipe below is an excellent place to start.

Pour the boiled water into a heatproof container (about 20 x 30cm/ 8 x 12in) that will snugly hold the fish in an even layer. Add the salt and stir until it has completely dissolved. When the water is cool enough to hold your finger in for 5 seconds without discomfort, lay the fish in the container, so there is as little overlap as possible. Nestle the celery, lemon peel, herbs and peppercorns around the fish, cover with a clean tea towel and leave to brine at room temperature for 15 minutes.

Meanwhile, make a start on the beans. Toss the shallot in a small bowl with the vinegar, sugar and ¼ teaspoon salt to lightly pickle. Set aside.

Bring a pan of salted water to the boil over a high heat. Add the beans and return the pan to the boil. Cook for 4 minutes, then drain in a colander. Fill the saucepan with cold water and submerge the beans under the water to stop them cooking and preserve their bright green colour. Set aside.

Melt the butter in a small saucepan over a medium heat, then cook until the butter begins to foam and turn a couple of shades darker, tilting and swirling the pan so you can see the butter changing colour as it cooks under the foam. When the butter has browned and smells nutty, about 5 minutes, remove from the heat and use a wooden spoon to loosen the solids from the base of the pan.

Browned butter can continue to cook for longer than you think –
it's only when it tastes bitter that it has gone too far. Set aside
2 tablespoons of the brown butter for the fish and leave the rest in
the pan for the beans, off the heat.

Next, cook the fish. Lift the fish out of the brine and pat dry. Spread
the flour out on a large plate and season generously with black
pepper. Put the fish on the flour and turn until coated on both sides.

Put two plates in a low oven (50°C/122°F) to warm. Heat a knob
of butter and a glug of oil in a large, heavy-based frying pan over a
medium heat until the butter melts and starts to bubble. The base of
the pan should be coated in a layer of fat to help crisp the fish skin
and prevent it sticking. Arrange the fish, two fillets at a time, skin-
side down, in the pan and cook, without disturbing for 4 minutes.
Use a spatula to gently turn the fish over and cook for another 90
seconds. Keep the two cooked fillets warm on your prewarmed
plates, in the low oven, while you cook the other two.

Finally, finish the beans. Return the pan with most of the brown
butter to a gentle heat. Stir through the beans for 3–4 minutes until
warmed through, then remove from the heat and season with a
pinch of salt. Add the pickled shallots, 1 tablespoon of the pickling
liquid, the almonds and chopped parsley. Taste and add more salt
and/or pepper until it tastes just right to you.

Serve the fish on the warmed plates with the reserved brown butter
drizzled over the top and the beans and lemon wedges alongside.

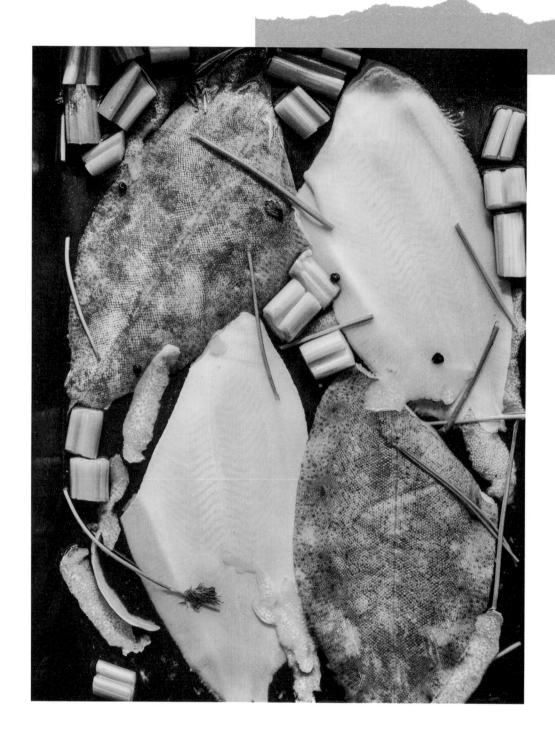

Citrus + bitter leaf salad with ricotta

Salad sitrws a dail chwerw gyda ricotta

🕐 Prep time: 25 minutes, plus
15 minutes brining
Cook time: 35 minutes

🍴 4 as a starter or side

This salad of grown-up flavours is worthy of celebrations and one we love to eat at Christmas, when blood oranges are in season. This recipe involves brining both the bitter leaves and the citrus, making for a dish that is sweet, salty and bitter, tempered by the creamy ricotta. It's a special starter or can be made into a more substantial meal with crusty bread and warmed-through grains served alongside.

For the brine
200ml/7fl oz boiled, slightly cooled water
1½ tsp finer flaked sea salt

For the salad
250g/9oz ricotta
1 head purple radicchio
1 head endive
1 orange
1 lemon
50g/1¾oz butter
2½ tbsp caster sugar
1 tsp red wine vinegar
¼ tsp freshly grated nutmeg
    (or ⅛ tsp ground nutmeg)

To serve
Handful of pomegranate seeds
1 orange, skin and pith removed and
    flesh cut into wedges
Thyme sprigs (optional)

Preheat the oven to 200°C/180°C fan/400°F/Gas 6.

Lay a cheesecloth or clean tea towel over a colander suspended over a bowl. Drain the ricotta in the centre of the cloth for at least an hour to concentrate the flavour and remove as much of the liquid as possible while you prepare the rest.

Combine the water and salt for the brine together in a jug and stir until the salt has dissolved. Cut the radicchio into six wedges lengthways through the root and the endive into four wedges through the root. Arrange the radicchio and endive wedges together in a container (about 20 x 30cm/8 x 12in) just large enough to hold them snugly in an even layer and pour over half of the brine. Using a very sharp knife, slice the orange and lemon into 2–4mm/¹⁄₁₆–⅛ in rounds, discarding the seeds and the tops and tails of the fruit so only the fleshy part is in rounds. Place the orange and lemon slices together in a medium bowl and cover with the remaining brine. Place a weight, such as a clean bowl or plate on top of the oranges to weigh them down. Leave the leaves and citrus for 15 minutes, turning the bitter leaves halfway through.

Drain the leaves and oranges and pat dry. Heat a quarter of the butter in a 28cm/11in ovenproof sauté pan over a medium heat until melted. Add the bitter leaf wedges to the pan on one cut side. They should all nestle in snugly. Fry, without disturbing for 3 minutes, then carefully turn them over so that the other cut side is on the base of the pan. Dot over a quarter more of the butter so the leaves don't burn and cook for another 3 minutes. Using a spatula, lift onto a clean tray and set aside while you cook the citrus.

Melt the remaining butter in the same pan and add the citrus slices in an even layer so there's as little overlap as possible. Sprinkle over the sugar and reduce the heat to low. Cook for 3 minutes, before turning over and cooking for another 5–7 minutes until all the slices are sticky and translucent. Lift onto a plate and turn off the hob.

Return the leaves to the pan, fanning each wedge out so that they cover the base and sprinkle over the vinegar. Nestle the caramelised citrus among the wedges so they don't catch and burn in the oven (which they will do if they are all on top). Put the whole ricotta into the centre of the pan and grate or sprinkle over the nutmeg. Bake for 20 minutes, or until the ricotta is wobbly, then dot over the remaining fresh orange, pomegranate seeds and thyme, if you like, and serve while still warm.

Chicken wings

Adenydd cyw iâr

This recipe showcases chicken wings, often overlooked in favour of prime cuts. The brining gives juicy flesh with crispy skin, well worth the effort of planning ahead. You can serve them either straight up or toss them in this glaze, which is a favourite in our house.

For the brine

200g/7oz light muscovado
    sugar

300g/10½oz finer flaked
    sea salt

12 juniper berries

12 cloves

1 star anise

12 black peppercorns

4 fresh bay leaves

For the chicken wings

24 organic chicken wings

2 tbsp baking powder

2 handfuls of panko breadcrumbs

Pinch of finer flaked sea salt

Freshly ground black pepper

For the glaze (optional)

2 tbsp rendered chicken fat from a
    previous roast chicken, or butter

4 tbsp pomegranate molasses

4 tbsp gochujang chilli paste

2 garlic cloves, crushed

4 tbsp ketchup

4 tbsp light muscovado sugar

 1 hour 30 minutes, plus overnight brining

 4

First, make the brine. You may want to do this the night before cooking to allow time for it to cool. Put all the brine ingredients and 2 litres/70fl oz water into a large saucepan and heat, stirring, until the salt and sugar have dissolved. Remove the pan from the heat and leave to cool.

Put the cooled brine and chicken wings into a large non-reactive food container, cover and store in the fridge overnight.

The next day, preheat the oven to 140°C/120°C fan/275°F/Gas 1.

Remove the chicken wings from the brine and wash in cold water, then leave the wings to dry on a wire rack (you can dry with kitchen paper to speed up this process). Mix together the baking powder, breadcrumbs, salt and pepper in a large bowl, then toss the wings in the mixture. This will ensure that the wings will crisp up perfectly during cooking.

Arrange the wings in a single layer on two baking sheets and cook for 30 minutes. Increase the oven temperature to 200°C/180°C fan/400°F/Gas 6 and cook for another 30 minutes, or until golden brown all over.

About 10 minutes before the wings are ready, start to prepare the glaze, if using. Place all the ingredients for the glaze in a medium saucepan and stir over a medium heat until the sugar has dissolved.

Pour the glaze carefully into a large heatproof bowl, add the chicken wings and toss until coated. Be careful, this will be incredibly tasty and incredibly hot!

Serve with Bread + Butter Pickles (p.118), a fresh salad and plenty of cold beer and napkins.

Black pepper-brined corn on the cob with romesco

India corn drwy heli pupur du gyda romesco

🕐 Prep time: 20 minutes,
plus 30 minutes cooling and
brining
Cook time: 1 hour

🍴 4 as a side

Brining corn is an absolute game-changer. This extra effort will make their texture juicy and fresh, making it a lively side dish in a barbecue spread. The romesco makes more than you will need for this recipe, so store in an airtight container in the fridge for up to a week, then serve alongside chicken, fish and roasted vegetables or in sandwiches. You can make the romesco with jarred peppers, but if they are stored in vinegar, you may need to adjust the levels of sweetness and salt.

For the romesco

3 large red peppers

75g/2¾oz stale bread (preferably sourdough), torn into chunks

Leaves from 1 small bunch of parsley, picked (use the stalks for stock or in the base of soups and sauces)

75g/2¾oz almonds, toasted

1 garlic clove, peeled

3 tbsp extra virgin olive oil

2 tsp tomato purée

1 tsp sherry vinegar

1 tsp sweet smoked paprika

¼ tsp dried chilli flakes

½ tsp finer flaked sea salt

Honey, to taste (optional)

Finer flaked sea salt and freshly ground black pepper

For the corn

25g/1oz finer flaked sea salt

1 heaped tsp black peppercorns, roughly crushed

500ml/18fl oz hot water

2 corn on the cobs, halved around the middle

To serve

Salted butter

1 lime, cut into wedges

Preheat the oven to 200°C/180°C fan/400°F/Gas 6. Line a large baking sheet with a silicone mat or baking paper.

For the romesco, arrange the peppers on the lined baking sheet, then without oiling or seasoning, cook them on the middle shelf of the oven for 40–50 minutes, turning three times during cooking until they are charred in places and completely soft all over. Use a large spoon to lift the peppers into a large bowl and cover tightly with clingfilm (this will help to release the pepper skins and make for a more pleasing texture to the romesco). Leave for 30 minutes, or until cool enough to handle. You can cook the peppers up to 6 hours in advance, if you like.

Using clean hands, peel away the pepper skins and discard, along with as many seeds as you can (don't worry about a few rogue ones), and the stalks. Transfer the peeled peppers and any cooking liquid to a food processor with the remaining ingredients, except the honey, and pulse until it forms a chunky paste. Taste and add honey, if you like – this will depend partly on the natural sweetness from the peppers, then season with salt and pepper to taste. Transfer to an airtight container and store in the fridge for up to a week. Bring to room temperature 30 minutes before serving.

For the corn, put the salt, pepper and hot water into a large bowl and stir together until the salt has dissolved. Add the corn, cover with a clean tea towel and set aside for 30 minutes, turning once as it brines.

Preheat a barbeque or griddle pan to cook the corn.

Pat the corn dry and barbecue or griddle (brushing with oil before cooking if you are using a barbecue), turning frequently for about 5–8 minutes until tender and charred in places. Remove from the heat and serve with 1 heaped tablespoon of the romesco, a knob of salted butter and a squeeze of lime.

Grilled radishes

Rhuddygl wedi'i grilio

Prep time: 25 minutes, plus 1 hour soaking +
30 minutes brining. Cook time: 20 minutes

4 as a starter or side

This is a wonderful way to start a summer supper – not least because it looks incredibly beautiful. Radishes in our house are often eaten raw with butter, and, you guessed it, flaked sea salt, but occasionally we like to cook them for something different. Brining the radishes before grilling gives them a lovely texture and enhances their distinctive flavour. We serve them with this fresh almond sauce, which is a savoury revelation alongside the mellow, peppery radishes.

For the radishes
400g/14oz radishes
2 tbsp finer flaked sea salt
1 tbsp caster sugar
Juice and pared peel of 1 lemon
2 bay leaves
5 black peppercorns
1 tbsp extra virgin olive oil

For the almond sauce
50g/1¾oz blanched almonds
2 garlic cloves
2 anchovy fillets in oil
½ tsp Dijon mustard
Juice of 1 lemon
150ml/5floz extra virgin olive oil
Finer flaked sea salt and freshly ground
    black pepper

For the parsley salsa
1 small bunch of parsley, finely chopped
1 tsp capers, roughly chopped
Juice of ½ lemon
2 tbsp extra virgin olive oil
1 tbsp ice-cold water
½ tsp honey

Soak the almonds for the sauce in a medium heatproof bowl of hot water for 1 hour.

Meanwhile, separate the radish leaves from the roots, set the leaves aside and halve the radishes lengthways. Place the radishes in another medium heatproof bowl.

Pour 1 litre/35fl oz water into a large saucepan, add the salt, sugar, lemon juice and peel, bay leaves and peppercorns and bring to a simmer, stirring to ensure all the sugar and salt have dissolved. Bring the mixture to the boil and immediately remove the pan from the heat. Pour the brine over the radishes and leave for 30 minutes, or until the radishes have turned a vibrant pink and released some of their colour into the liquid.

Meanwhile, make the almond sauce. Drain the almonds, discard the soaking water and put the nuts in a blender with the garlic, anchovies, mustard and lemon juice. With the motor running slowly, gradually pour the oil in a thin, steady stream, then increase the speed to high and blend for 1 minute until smooth and thickened. Remove the lid, taste and adjust the seasoning with salt and pepper (it may not need any salt as the anchovies are salty). Cover and set aside.

Preheat the grill to medium and line a 20 x 30cm/8 x 12in roasting tin with foil. Lift the radishes and lemon peel out of the brining liquid with a slotted spoon (leaving the whole spices) and pat dry. Any leftover brining liquid can be used to brine other root vegetables. Arrange the radishes in a single layer in the prepared tin and drizzle with the oil. Toss with clean hands to coat, then grill for 15–20 minutes, turning once, until the radishes are wrinkled and tender to the point of a sharp knife.

Meanwhile, mix all the ingredients for the parsley salsa together in a small bowl. There is no need to season it with salt as the radishes and almond sauce are salty.

Spread the almond sauce over a small serving plate. Top with the roasted radishes and drizzle over the salsa. Serve with chunky bread for mopping up the almond sauce.

Spiced squash with tahini yogurt sauce

Pwmpen sbeislyd gyda saws iogwrt tahini

This is an unusual way of eating squash, but a delicious one. Brining it before griddling seasons it beautifully and changes the texture into something fresher than you'd expect. Take care when preparing the squash, as the size of the pieces are important – 1cm/½in slices gives the right amount of surface area for the brine to permeate the squash and ensures the pieces are tender throughout when cooked. This is lovely as it is as a light supper, or feel free to use some of the brine and vinegar to quickly pickle some onions to serve alongside couscous or flatbread for something more substantial.

For the squash

1 butternut squash (about 1kg/2lb 3¼oz), peeled and cut in half around the middle

30g/1oz finer flaked sea salt

2 tbsp soft light brown sugar

2 tbsp rice wine vinegar

12 black peppercorns

1 cinnamon stick

1 star anise

4 cardamom pods

1 fresh red chilli, pierced down one length with a sharp knife

Extra virgin olive oil, for brushing

½ small bunch of dill, leaves picked

Pangrattato (p.131), to serve (optional)

For the tahini + yogurt sauce

175ml/6fl oz Greek yogurt

5 tbsp tahini

1 tsp sea salt

2 tsp honey

Juice of ½ lemon

1 garlic clove, very finely chopped

 Prep time: 25 minutes, plus 1 ¼ hours brining
Cook time: 40 minutes

4–6

Slice the bulbous, bottom half of the squash in half lengthways and use a spoon to scoop out the seeds and discard them. Lay the flat side of the squash on a chopping board and use your sharpest knife to slice the squash into 1cm/½in crescents, transferring to a large heatproof bowl as you go. Repeat with the other half, then slice the top in half lengthways and slice into 1cm/½in half-moons, placing all the sliced pieces into the bowl.

Pour 2 litres/70fl oz water into a large saucepan with the salt, sugar, vinegar and spices, including the chilli. Bring to a simmer, then stir to dissolve the sugar and salt. Bring to the boil, then remove from the heat and pour the liquid and all the spices over the squash. Leave for 1¼ hours.

Preheat a low oven. Heat a griddle pan over a medium-high heat for at least 5 minutes until fiercely hot. Lift the squash out of the brining mixture with a slotted spoon and pat dry (any remaining mixture can be used to brine other root vegetables to season before roasting or grilling). Griddle the squash, in batches, for 8 minutes before turning over and cooking the other side for another 8 minutes, or until the squash is striped like a tiger all over. Brush each piece with olive oil and keep warm in the low oven while you cook the rest. Alternatively, brush the squash with oil and cook under a medium-high grill for 20 minutes, turning halfway through.

Meanwhile, whisk all the ingredients for the tahini and yogurt sauce together in a medium bowl until smooth. Loosen with 3–4 tablespoons water until the mixture resembles thickened cream. Taste and add more salt, honey or lemon, according to your preference.

Spread half the sauce on a platter, top with the cooked squash and drizzle over the remaining sauce. Scatter the dill leaves over the top and sprinkle with a generous serving spoon of the Pangrattato, if using.

Serve with flatbreads and a green salad, or couscous, finished with lemon juice, and a small bunch of chopped parsley and mint, for a more substantial meal.

PICKLING
+ FERMENTING

PICLO AC
EPLESU

Fermented chilli hot sauce

Saws poeth tsili eplesedig

This is a killer hot sauce, if we do say so ourselves. Cooking it briefly at the end brings all the flavours together and mellows some of the acidity that's been created by the fermentation. The hot sauce needs to ferment at room temperature for 1–2 weeks before it's ready to consume.

500ml/18fl oz boiling water

20g/¾oz flaked sea salt

10 fresh red chillies (about 150g/5¼oz), cut into 1cm/½in pieces, but seeds retained

1 thumb-sized piece of fresh root ginger, peeled and finely chopped

1 banana shallot, roughly chopped

4 garlic cloves, peeled

3 fresh bay leaves

¼ tsp fennel seeds

1 tbsp extra virgin olive oil

1 tsp caster sugar

Prep time: 10 minutes
Cook time: 10 minutes, plus 1–2 weeks fermenting

Makes 300ml/10½fl oz jar

Pour the boiling water into a large heatproof jug, add the salt and stir until the salt dissolves. Cover with a clean tea towel and leave the liquid to cool until warm.

Pack all the remaining ingredients, except the oil and sugar, into a sterilised 1 litre/35fl oz jar. Pour over the brine and cover with a lid. Set the jar aside at room temperature for at least a week to ferment, or up to two weeks for a stronger flavour. The liquid in the jar may turn cloudy after a few days – this is completely normal and safe, and just means the lactic acid is working and fermentation is taking place.

Drain the ingredients through a sieve suspended over a jug to keep the liquid. Blitz the chilli mixture, bay leaves and all, in a blender or food processor until just smooth, loosening with 4 tablespoons of the brine and scraping down the sides a few times to make sure the mixture is as evenly blended as possible.

Heat the oil in a small saucepan over a medium-low heat, add the blitzed chilli sauce and the sugar and cook until there is almost no liquid left in the pan and the sauce has taken on a bright orange tint. Transfer to a sterilised 300ml/10½fl oz jar, seal with a lid and store in the fridge. Enjoy within six months.

Ideas for serving

• Use in the Fermented Chilli + Spring Onion Fishcakes on p.122.

• Serve alongside poached eggs.

• Swirl into soups, such as carrot or sweet potato, for a lift.

• Dot onto raw oysters.

• Stir into mayonnaise to serve alongside burgers, chips or chicken sandwiches.

Straight-up sauerkraut

Sauerkraut syml

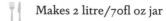

🕐 20 minutes, plus 5+ days fermentation

🍴 Makes 2 litre/70fl oz jar

How could we write a book on sea salt and not include a recipe for this most satisfying of staples? If you've never made it before, now is your chance. Making sauerkraut is such a tactile process – you really feel *you* have made it. When choosing vegetables for preserving, look and feel for freshness and choose vegetables that feel heavy for their size. If you've got one, we recommend using a mandolin for shredding the cabbage as it gives such a fine result.

1 white cabbage, outer leaves reserved and remaining leaves finely shredded (750g/26½oz prepared weight)

25g/1oz flaked sea salt, plus 1 tsp extra, if needed

6 juniper berries (optional)

½ tsp caraway seeds (optional)

100ml/3½fl oz boiled water (optional)

Note
Lacto-fermented vegetables have a flavour that develops and intensifies over time. After five days of fermentation, taste a little of the kraut, then taste every day for up to a month until you're happy, and then move to the fridge. The important thing is that the weight of salt should be 4 per cent that of the cabbage for safe and effective fermentation (so 1kg/2lb 3¼oz cabbage would require 40g/1½oz flaked sea salt. If you end up with more or less cabbage, that's fine, just adjust the amount of salt in the recipe.

Put the cabbage and salt into a large, clean bowl and toss to combine. Using clean hands, rub the cabbage and salt together, using a motion like rubbing together butter and flour for a crumble topping. Continue for 10 minutes to create a brine from the cabbage and salt. We find this quite meditative and try to use a shallow bowl to rest our arms on the side of.

If your wrists begin to hurt, rub as much salt as you can into the cabbage, then cover with a smaller clean bowl weighed down, for example with a pestle and mortar or clean stone. Leave for 1 hour, by which time more of the liquid should have been drawn out of the cabbage.

When the liquid in the base of the bowl pools around the base of the cabbage, toss through the juniper berries and caraway seeds, if using. Begin to pack the cabbage into a sterilised 1 litre/35fl oz preserving jar. Working in handfuls, push the cabbage down using a tight fist, to pack it down as firmly as possible. After a couple of handfuls, the brine should begin to rise above the cabbage when pushed down. Continue to fill the jar using up all of the cabbage and pouring over any remaining brine. You should be left with a few centimetres of space between the surface of the brine and the top of the jar. This is important to allow any air created by fermentation the ability to escape. If you are short on space, divide the cabbage and brine between two sterilised jars.

Take one (or two if using two jars) of the reserved cabbage leaves and press down over the cabbage. Place a clean stone or small jar on the leaf to weigh the shredded cabbage down below the surface of a brine. If the brine doesn't cover the cabbage completely, mix the boiled water with the extra teaspoon of salt and pour over the cabbage to cover. Cover with a lid and set aside at room temperature to ferment for five days, opening the jar every day to release any trapped air. Begin to taste after five days and ferment for up to four weeks until the desired flavour is achieved.

Store in the fridge for up to six months.

Ideas for serving
- Use in the Reuben Sandwich p.121.
- Stir into a potato rosti mix before cooking.
- Add 2 tablespoons to finely chopped, sautéed garlicky mushrooms to use as a dumpling filling.

Spiced tomato chutney

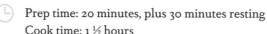

Catwad tomato sbeislyd

We're going to make a bold claim with this recipe – it might be our favourite chutney of all time. It's best made at the end of a hot summer, when it feels like the trugs of tomatoes will never stop coming. Don't be put off by the lengthy ingredients list – many are likely to be in your spice cupboard already and don't be tempted to skip toasting the spices as this will really amplify the flavours. Opening the chutney too early can result in a harsh, vinegar-forward flavour, so be patient. The resting time will help to develop the flavour and balance everything out.

2.25kg/4lb 15oz ripe red tomatoes (any variety), roughly chopped into 2cm/¾in pieces

3 eating apples, cored and cut into 1cm/½in pieces

2 white onions, finely sliced

2 tbsp flaked sea salt, plus 1 tsp

1 thumb-sized piece of fresh root ginger, peeled and grated

525ml/17¾fl oz apple cider vinegar or white wine vinegar

5 cloves

7 cardamom pods

1 tbsp black onion (nigella) seeds

2 tsp cumin seeds

2 tsp coriander seeds

2 tsp yellow mustard seeds

1 cinnamon stick

1 star anise

1 tsp ground turmeric

½ tsp dried chilli flakes

5 fresh bay leaves

425g/15oz caster sugar

Prep time: 20 minutes, plus 30 minutes resting
Cook time: 1 ½ hours

Makes 5 x 350ml/12fl oz jars

Put the tomatoes, apples and onions into a large bowl with 2 tablespoons of the salt. Toss together, then set aside for 30 minutes. The salt will draw the liquid from the tomatoes and begin to intensify their flavour straight away.

Tip the contents of the bowl into a large saucepan, including any liquid in the base of the bowl. Add the ginger and vinegar and bring to the boil. Reduce the heat and simmer gently for 1 hour, or until there is almost no liquid left in the pan.

Measure all of the whole spices into a bowl. Heat a dry frying pan over a medium heat until hot, then add all the spices and toast for 2–3 minutes until deeply fragrant, and you hear the mustard seeds popping. Toasting the spices like this will release their aromatic oils and amplify their flavour. Stir the toasted spices, ground turmeric, chilli flakes and bay leaves into the tomato mixture, along with the sugar and remaining 1 teaspoon of salt. The sugar and salt will draw more liquid from the tomato mixture and help it to turn a deeper shade of red. Cook for 20–30 minutes until the mixture is a few shades of red darker and glossy. The cooking time will depend on the water content of the tomatoes and their ripeness.

Spoon the hot chutney into five hot sterilised 350ml/12fl oz jars, seal with the lids and turn the jars upside down to sterilise the lids. Store in a cool, dark place for at least three weeks before opening. The jars will keep in the cupboard for up to six months. After opening, store in the fridge and consume within a month.

Ideas for serving

• Perk up a ploughman's sandwich with a slick on buttered bread.

• Pair with a buttery paneer curry.

• Spread over peanut butter on toast for a modern peanut butter and jelly sandwich.

• Serve alongside a lovely cheese board.

Preserved limes

Leim cadw

Preserving limes changes their character entirely, into something nearly sherbety, with a distinct flavour. Amazingly, all you need is salt and time. It's best to use organic, unwaxed limes here, as pesticides can affect the flavour, which would be a shame after being patient for all that time!

12 limes, rinsed
7 tbsp flaked sea salt
1 small green chilli, halved lengthways
1 tsp coriander seeds
12 black peppercorns

15 minutes,
plus 4 weeks fermenting

Makes 1 litre/35fl oz jar

Scrub the six freshest-looking limes dry with a clean tea towel and cut a deep cross in each, coming to within 2cm/¾in of the base, to open up the fruit but not to separate it into pieces. Spoon 1 tablespoon of the salt into the cut centre of each lime. Press down into a sterilised 1 litre/35fl oz preserving jar, nestling the chilli and spices among the fruit as you go. Scatter over the remaining salt and use a fist to press the fruit down to the base of the jar. Squeeze over the juice of the remaining limes. Cover with a lid and leave at room temperature for 24 hours.

After 24 hours, uncover and press down on the fruit with a fist to extract as much liquid as possible. Cover with a lid and repeat the following day.

Keep the preserved limes in a cool, dark place for four weeks, turning the jar to rest upside down every other day, to ensure each piece of fruit has time under the brine. Keep at room temperature.

Before using the limes in any of your cooking, discard the flesh and pith (which are too salty) and slice or chop the skins.

Ideas for serving

• Blitz into salsas to spoon onto tacos or roasted vegetables.
• Finely chop with herbs and mix with oil and fresh lime juice to drizzle over cooked prawns or flaky white fish.
• Tuck strips under the skin of chicken before roasting.
• Finely chop and stir into chickpea stew.
• Toss through noodles with tahini and greens.

Overknight courgette pickles

We love these pickles tumbled through warm roasted aubergines and red peppers, but really they are a welcome addition to any sandwich, toastie or barbecue spread. Slicing the courgettes into ribbons is easiest with fresh, firm courgettes and a sharp potato peeler or mandolin. Salting helps remove moisture from the courgette before you start pickling, to make sure they have the perfect crunch we all know and love.

2 large courgettes (about 600g/1lb 5oz), shaved lengthways (cut the courgettes in half around the middle if the length is awkward)

2 shallots, finely sliced

4 spring onions, finely sliced

3 tsp flaked sea salt

3 basil sprigs, leaves picked

175ml/6fl oz apple cider or white wine vinegar

60g/2¼oz caster sugar

5 black peppercorns

1 tsp black onion (nigella) seeds

1 small fresh red or green chilli, finely sliced

Prep time: 10 minutes, plus 6 hours draining
Cook time: 5 minutes, plus 24 hours resting

Makes 1 litre/35fl oz jar

Toss the courgettes, shallots and spring onions together in a large bowl. Add the salt and, using clean hands, toss the vegetables to combine. Pour the vegetables into a colander and suspend it over the bowl to catch any liquid that drains from the vegetables. Cover and leave in the fridge for at least 6 hours, or overnight.

After the draining time, rinse the vegetables in the colander under cold running water for at least a minute, tossing a couple of times to expose all the vegetables to the water. Shake well and pat the vegetables dry with a clean tea towel.

Pack the vegetables into a sterilised 1 litre/35fl oz jar with a lid, nestling the basil among the vegetables as you go.

Heat the vinegar, sugar and 160ml/5½fl oz water in a saucepan over a low heat until the sugar dissolves. Add the peppercorns and black onion seeds and bring the mixture to the boil. Stir in the chilli and boil for 1 minute before carefully pouring the hot liquid over the vegetables in the jar. Cover with the sterilised lid and leave to cool before transferring to the fridge. Leave to pickle in the fridge for 24 hours before opening. The vegetables will keep in the fridge for up to a month.

Ideas for serving

• Serve alongside grilled or barbecued white fish or halloumi.

• Toss through cooked rice or lentils and drizzle with garlicky herb sauce or salsa verde.

• Add to a falafel wrap.

Lemon + thyme kohlrabi pickles

Piclau kohlrabi lemon a theim

Kohlrabi can sometimes get lost among other ingredients, but this preserve celebrates its fresh flavour, with lemon and thyme adding some fragrance. That said, if it's tricky to find, we've also tried this recipe with baby turnips and parsnips and it worked beautifully. Use a mandolin or a really sharp knife – the success of this recipe relies on all of the pieces being as uniform and thin as possible. Try the pickle in slaws, savoury pancake batters, smoked salmon and cream cheese in a bagel or in wraps and burgers for a similar contrast to pickled gherkins and sauerkraut. We've included a killer cheese toastie opposite, as it really makes a hero of the pickle.

2 kohlrabi (about 500g/1lb 2oz), peeled and cut into matchsticks, or use the same weight of light, sweet root vegetables such as parsnip, turnip or swede

1 small white onion, peeled and finely sliced

350ml/12fl oz apple cider vinegar

1 tbsp flaked sea salt

2 tbsp caster sugar

Pared peel of 1 lemon

5 thyme or lemon thyme sprigs

1 tsp yellow mustard seeds

Prep time: 15 minutes
Cook time: 5 minutes, plus 3 days resting

Makes 3 x 400ml/14fl oz jars

Mix the kohlrabi and onion in a large bowl to combine, then pack the vegetables into three 400ml/14fl oz hot sterilised jars, or use one larger (1.5 litre/52¾fl oz) jar, if you prefer.

Pour the vinegar into a large saucepan and add 350ml/12fl oz water and the salt together with the remaining ingredients, except the vegetables. Heat gently over a medium heat until the salt and sugar dissolve, then bring to the boil. Immediately remove the pan from the heat and carefully pour the hot liquid over the kohlrabi mixture in the jars to cover, making sure the vegetables are submerged. Check that there is a roughly even distribution of aromatics (thyme, lemon and mustard seeds) between the jars. Seal with the sterilised lids and leave to cool.

When cool, transfer to the fridge. Leave for at least three days before opening and consume within three months.

For the grilled cheese sandwich

Grating the cheese really finely helps it to melt evenly – it will look like a lot before it's cooked but will melt down to the perfect amount. The kohlrabi provides a contrast similar to fermented vegetables or gherkins, but if you have a sweet tooth, a dollop of the Spiced Tomato Chutney (p.104) wouldn't go amiss here alongside the hot mustard.

2 thick slices of rustic white bread, such as sourdough

Butter, for spreading and frying

1 tbsp Dijon mustard

2 tbsp Lemon + Thyme Kohlrabi Pickles (see opposite), patted dry on kitchen paper

45g/1½oz strong Cheddar cheese, finely grated

4 dill sprigs, leaves picked

10 minutes

Makes 1

Preheat the grill to medium-high and heat a large ovenproof or cast-iron pan over a medium heat.

Spread each slice of bread with butter on one side, then spread the mustard on one of the slices and top with the kohlrabi and cheese.

Heat a knob, about 25g/1oz, of butter in the pan until melted and bubbling. Arrange the cheese-topped bread, cheesy-side up, in the pan, then lay the other piece of buttered bread alongside, buttered side down, and toast for 1 minute, before placing the pan under the grill for about 5 minutes, or until the cheese is melted and has begun to darken.

Remove the pan from the grill and return to the hob over a medium heat. Scatter the dill evenly over the cheese, then carefully lift the lightly buttered bread and lay it over the cheesy slice. Toast on the hob, pressing down occasionally with a spatula for 2–3 minutes on each side until crisp and dark golden. Serve immediately.

Constraints
Make You
Interesting,

Black
garlic
ketchup

Black garlic

🕐 15–20 days   🍴 Makes 20– 30 heads

When you cook garlic extremely slowly the enzymes that give it its sharpness break down. Amino acids and sugars react with heat to give a distinct flavour that is insanely delicious – think of a toasted sourdough loaf, browned cookies or the edge of lasagne. The rawness of garlic becomes something much more mellow.

You can buy black garlic, but experimenting with making your own is a lot of fun. Over the course of four weeks your cloves will go from snow white to intense, rich balsamic black. It's really simple to make, especially if you have a slow cooker (worth noting we kept ours in the shed for the duration as things do get quite garlicky in the process).

20–30 good-quality garlic heads

You need to make sure the garlic doesn't burn so the easiest thing to do is take a bit of tinfoil, scrunch it up and place it in the bottom of the slow cooker. Put down a couple of sheets of kitchen paper and then add in a layer of garlic bulbs. Put another few sheets of kitchen paper on top – they prevent the garlic from getting too dry.

Switch your slow cooker to its 'keep warm' setting.

After 5–6 days check the garlic isn't drying out too much, you don't want the bulbs to be crispy. If they are starting to look that way, moisten the kitchen paper.

After 10–11 days slice a bulb open and have a look. You should see it starting to turn black. Depending on the ambient temperature and humidity it might be done. Anything from 14–20 days and it will reach perfect sticky blackness.

Seal all your black garlic cloves in a sterilised jar and they'll keep for up to a year.

Black garlic ketchup

🕐 5 minutes   🍴 Makes 20ml

40–50 black garlic cloves (see above)
1 small yellow onion, roughly chopped
30g/1oz demerara sugar
4 tbsp balsamic vinegar
6 tbsp olive oil
4 tbsp apple cider vinegar
¼ tsp fine sea salt

Note
Keeps for one month – once open keep it in the fridge.

This ketchup is an essential at barbecues, but really, a dollop of it will make pretty much anything better, whether it be a scallop or a sausage, a fried egg or a bowl of rice. If you've made your black garlic with the method above and it's been a few months then the cloves may be a little dry; we want them moist. You can revive them by putting into cold water for a few hours. Using a powerful blender will give the best texture.

Put all the ingredients in a strong blender, with 40ml /1½fl oz cold water. Pulse until you have a smooth sauce. You may need to add a splash more water to loosen it up depending on how dry the black garlic is. Pour into a sterilised bottle.

Cabbage, carrot, ginger + garlic sauerkraut

Sauerkraut bresych, moron, sinsir a garlleg

This funky, slightly spicy sauerkraut with an incredibly savoury flavour from the garlic is perfect added to Asian-inspired stir-fries or generously filled wraps. We've given weights for the vegetables here, as the ratio of vegetable to salt needs to be quite specific for successful fermentation. It will take anywhere from five days to four weeks to ferment, and it's ready to consume.

1 small white cabbage, outer leaves reserved and remaining cabbage finely shredded (500g/1lb 2oz prepared weight)

28g/1oz flaked sea salt

1 fennel bulb, core discarded and finely sliced (about 250g/9oz prepared weight)

2 carrots, peeled then peeled into ribbons (about 250g/9oz prepared weight)

4 garlic cloves, finely sliced

1 thumb-sized piece of fresh root ginger, peeled and finely chopped

200ml/7fl oz boiled water

Prep time: 20 minutes, plus 5 days – 4 weeks preserving

Makes about 1kg/2lb 3¼oz or a 2 litre/70fl oz jar

Prepare the cabbage by rubbing with 20g/¾oz of the salt as described on p.103, until the liquid in the bowl makes up a third of the volume.

Toss the cabbage and brine mixture with the remaining ingredients, except the boiled water, in a large bowl. Pack the ingredients into a large, sterilised (2 litre/70fl oz) preserving or kilner jar and press down with a fist to compact the vegetables tightly and extract as much of the brine over the vegetables as possible.

Mix the boiled water and remaining 8g/⅓oz salt togther in a large jug, then pour this over the vegetables to cover. Weigh down the vegetables with a reserved cabbage leaf, then use a weight such as a clean stone or small jar on top. Cover with the lid and leave to ferment at room temperature for five days, opening the jar every day to release any trapped air. Begin to taste after five days and leave for up to four weeks until the desired flavour is achieved. Store in the fridge for up to six months.

Ideas for serving

• Add a few forkfuls to a vegetable stir-fry 2 minutes before the end of the cooking time.

• Add to a cheese toastie.

• Add to a baked potato with baked beans.

• Chop it into a tomato salsa to eat alongside burritos or nachos.

• Serve alongside a fried egg on toast.

Pickled mango hot sauce

Everyone in our house is happy when we have a few jars of this in the cupboard – it's a beautiful marinade for chicken or tofu. Curing the mango first really brings out the sunshine flavour. If you prefer a less spicy condiment, remove the seeds from the chillies.

4 ripe mangoes, peeled, stoned and cut into 2cm/¾in cubes

4 fresh red chillies, cut into rough 2cm/¾in rounds

40g/1½oz flaked sea salt

2 tbsp vegetable oil

6 garlic cloves, finely chopped

1 tbsp black mustard seeds

1 tsp fenugreek seeds

2 tsp ground cumin

2 tsp ground coriander

1 tsp ground turmeric

1 tsp ground cardamom

1 tsp ground ginger

100ml/3½fl oz apple cider vinegar or white wine vinegar

3 tbsp dark brown sugar

Prep time: 10 minutes, plus 24 hours curing
Cook time: 20 minutes

Makes 4 x 400ml/14fl oz jars

Put the mango and chilli into a large bowl, add the salt and toss together. Cover with a clean tea towel and leave to cure in the fridge for 24 hours.

The next day, heat the oil in a large saucepan over a medium heat, add the garlic, mustard seeds and fenugreek seeds and fry for 2 minutes, stirring frequently, until the mustard seeds start to pop. Add the remaining (ground) spices and 1 tablespoon water and cook for 1–2 minutes until everything is fragrant and the liquid has evaporated.

Pour the mango and chilli mixture, including all the liquid, into the saucepan and stir to combine. Add the vinegar and sugar and bring to the boil. Reduce the heat and simmer for 15 minutes. Remove from the heat and leave to cool for 10 minutes, then blitz with a stick blender until smooth. Spoon the sauce into four sterilised 400ml/14fl oz jars and cover with the sterilised lids. Leave to cool before storing in the fridge. It is ready to eat immediately after cooking. The sauce will keep in the fridge for up to three months or a week after opening.

Ideas for serving

• Serve as a dip for samosas or bhajis.

• Use as a marinade for grilled chicken or tofu.

• Spoon into sandwiches and wraps as you would chutneys and pickles.

• Whisk with oil and lime to thin and drizzle over grilled fish or noodle dishes.

• Spoon into tacos alongside black beans and roasted vegetables.

• Mix with yogurt as a simple dip for crudités.

Bread + butter pickles

Piclau bara menyn

We've been making some version of these traditional pickles for generations in our family, and they will often be on the lunch table to liven up leftovers and sandwiches. Ideally, you'd use a mandolin to slice the onions as finely as possible, but just remember to always use the guard to protect your fingertips. Celery salt adds something savoury here, but a finer flaked sea salt would do the job if you don't have it.

2 cucumbers (about 350g/12¼oz each), finely sliced

1 onion, finely sliced

25g/1oz flaked sea salt

300ml/10fl oz apple cider vinegar

200g/7oz soft light brown sugar

8 black peppercorns

1 x 3cm/1¼in piece turmeric root, peeled and sliced into 5mm/¼in rounds (or 1 tsp ground turmeric)

1 tbsp yellow mustard seeds

1 heaped tsp celery salt

Prep time: 15 minutes, plus 2 hours draining
Cook time: 10 minutes, plus 3 days resting

Makes 4 x 350ml/12fl oz jars

Layer the sliced cucumber and onion in a large bowl, scattering with the flaked sea salt as you go, until all the salt is used up. Weigh the vegetables down with a bowl that will fit snugly over the mixing bowl and leave in the fridge for at least 2 hours, or overnight.

Drain the cucumber and onions in a colander and rinse well under cold running water for at least 1 minute, or until the cucumbers taste only vaguely salty. Squeeze any excess water from the vegetables using clean hands. Loosely pack the cucumber and onion mixture into four sterilised 350ml/12fl oz screw-top jars.

Heat the vinegar, sugar and spices, including the celery salt, together in a large saucepan over a medium-low heat until the sugar has dissolved. Don't stir. Bring to the boil, then immediately remove from the heat and carefully pour the hot liquid over the cucumber mixture in the jars to cover. Seal with the lids and turn the jars over to sterilise the lids. Leave to cool completely.

Leave the pickles for three days at room temperature before eating. They can be kept unopened in the cupboard for up to six months. After opening, store in the fridge and consume within a month.

Ideas for serving

• Use on flatbreads with cream cheese and fresh dill.

• Serve alongside hot-smoked salmon.

• Mix with finely chopped chilli and toasted sesame seeds to serve alongside a Japanese-inspired stir-fry.

• Use as the perfect condiment at a barbecue.

Reuben sandwich

Brechdan Reuben

 30 minutes

 2 generously

An indulgent sandwich that we first tasted, of course, in New York City, when visiting American customers. As classic as the yellow taxi itself, this recipe makes a generous sandwich, but if you want to make a few, then any leftover dressing perks up an avocado or chicken wrap no end. It's the kind of sandwich we like to eat between Christmas and New Year, when no one really knows what day it is, but everyone knows what they want in their sandwich. The veggies among us will be pleased to know that it is still delicious without the beef and Worcestershire sauce, perhaps add an extra slice or two of cheese instead.

Have a dry frying pan ready to toast the sandwich. Mix all the dressing ingredients together and season to taste.

Butter each slice of bread on both sides – you may find it easier to do this on baking paper. Place the salt beef on a piece of the buttered bread and top with the cheese and Sauerkraut. Spread the Russian dressing over the other slice and place it onto the Sauerkraut.

Heat a dry pan on a medium heat. Fry the sandwich in the hot pan, turning it to brown on each side, until the cheese has melted. Serve with Bread + Butter Pickles or Overnight Courgette Pickles and plenty of cold beer.

For the Russian dressing

2 tbsp mayonnaise (p.38)

2 tbsp tomato ketchup
(you can use Bloody Mary ketchup for extra zing)

2 tbsp horseradish sauce

Generous dash of Fermented Chilli Hot Sauce (p.100)

Generous dash of Worcestershire sauce

2 tsp finely chopped shallot

1 tbsp Bread + Butter Pickles (p.118), chopped, or 2 finely chopped cornichons, plus extra, to serve (optional)

Finer flaked sea salt and freshly ground black pepper

For the sandwich

Butter, for spreading

4 slices of light rye bread

3–4 slices of Salt Beef (p.134), or corned beef

4 slices of Swiss cheese, such as Gruyère

3–4 tbsp Straight-up Sauerkraut (p.103)

Overnight Courgette Pickles (p.107), to serve (optional)

Note
Choose a sourdough rye if you can as it will make a difference (not the German-style rye bread). You can make the dressing more piquant by dialling up the pickles, or hotter by adding more horseradish or hot sauce. It's the perfect showcase for the pickles and ferments in this book.

Fermented chilli + spring onion fishcakes

Cacennau pysgod gyda tsili eplesedig a shibwns

These satisfying little fishcakes make the most of the Fermented Chilli Hot Sauce on p.100, as well as a sustainable catch. Smoked mackerel has the added bonus of a stronger flavour, meaning you need less of it. You can also make them vegetarian by omitting the fish, adding a little more cheese and topping with a perfect fried egg. Don't be tempted to skip the fridge resting time as the fishcakes won't hold together in the pan. Tasting is important as you cook here – the mackerel, cheese and hot sauce are sources of saltiness, so you'll need less seasoning.

500g/1lb 2oz floury potatoes, scrubbed but unpeeled (or use the same weight of leftover mashed potatoes)

2 tbsp finer flaked sea salt

1 tbsp extra virgin olive oil

1 bunch of spring onions, white and light green parts finely sliced

250g/9oz hot-smoked mackerel fillets, skin removed and fillets flaked

50g/1¾oz mature Cheddar cheese, finely grated

2 tbsp Fermented Chilli Hot Sauce (p.100), plus extra to serve

½ small bunch of dill, leaves picked and finely chopped

100ml/3½fl oz whole milk

75g/2¾oz panko breadcrumbs

Vegetable or groundnut oil, for shallow-frying

Flaked sea salt and freshly ground black pepper

1 lemon, cut into wedges, to serve

Prep time: 20 minutes, plus 1 hour chilling
Cook time: 50 minutes – 1 hour and 20 minutes

4

Put the potatoes into a large saucepan, cover with double the volume of cold water and bring to the boil. Add the salt and cook the potatoes for 30–60 minutes until they are completely tender all the way through when the point of a sharp knife is inserted. If the potatoes are different sizes, remove any that are cooked through to drain before the other, larger ones are completely tender. Drain the potatoes in a colander and allow the steam to evaporate for 15 minutes.

When the potatoes are cool enough to handle, use clean hands to peel off the skins and discard. Put the potatoes into a large shallow bowl and mash with a fork until smooth. Heat the olive oil in a small frying pan over a medium heat, add the spring onions and fry for 2 minutes until completely soft and translucent. Add to the potato mixture along with the mackerel, cheese, hot sauce and dill. Season with salt and pepper to taste. Set aside.

Pour the milk into a shallow bowl and scatter the breadcrumbs over a large plate. Line a baking sheet that will fit in the fridge with baking paper or a silicone mat.

Using clean hands, shape 90–100g/3¼–3½oz of the fish mix into a round burger. Dip into the milk, then carefully turn over in the breadcrumbs to coat. Put onto the lined sheet and repeat with the remaining fishcake mixture, milk and breadcrumbs. Chill in the fridge for 1 hour. At this stage, they can be frozen on a tray for up to three months, or cooked the same day. If cooking from frozen, allow the fishcakes to defrost completely at room temperature before frying.

Heat enough vegetable oil to coat the base of a frying pan over a medium heat. Add the chilled fishcakes in batches, leaving plenty of space in the pan for flipping, and shallow-fry for 5–7 minutes on each side until crisp and golden. Keep the cooked fishcakes warm in a low oven while you cook the rest.

Serve the fishcakes immediately with lemon wedges, a crisp green salad and extra fermented chilli sauce on the side.

CURING

HALEN MÔR

Rhubarb + goat's cheese tart

Tarten riwbob a chaws gafr

🕐 Prep time: 25 minutes, plus 20 minutes curing
Cook time: 1 ½ hours

🍴 4–6

For the pastry

225g/8oz plain flour, sifted

110g/3¾oz butter, chilled and diced,
plus extra for greasing

1 medium egg yolk

20g/¾oz Parmesan cheese,
finely grated

2–4 tbsp ice-cold water

½ tsp finer flaked sea salt

Freshly ground black pepper

For the cured rhubarb

2 slim rhubarb stalks (about 150g/5¼oz),
sliced in half lengthways, then cut
into 1cm/½in pieces

5g/¹∕₈oz finer flaked sea salt

25g/1oz caster sugar

2 lemon thyme sprigs

½ tsp fennel seeds

For the tart filling

25g/1oz butter

4 onions, finely sliced

2 medium eggs, beaten

100ml/3½fl oz double cream

Leaves from a small bunch of parsley,
finely chopped

½ tsp Dijon mustard

80g/2¾oz fresh young rindless
goat's cheese

3 lemon thyme sprigs (or use thyme
leaves and grated lemon zest)

Sea salt and freshly ground black pepper

This is a tart so beautiful you'll want to frame it. Curing the rhubarb in a sugar and salt mixture helps to tone down its sharpness, while preserving its bright, vibrant flavour. You can cure, rinse and dry this in advance, storing it overnight in the fridge, before bringing it altogether. If you have ever struggled to roll out pastry but love the incredible texture of a really short crust, this is the recipe for you – freezing and grating the dough is absolutely foolproof. You can also make the dough and store it in the fridge overnight, then pop it into the freezer for 30 minutes just before you want to bake it.

Start by making the pastry. Pulse the flour and butter together in a food processor until the mixture resembles breadcrumbs. Add the egg yolk and Parmesan and pulse a couple of times to combine. Pour in the water, 1 tablespoon at a time, until the mixture comes together when you pinch it between your fingers. You may not need all the water. Add the salt and pepper and pulse again to combine. Transfer to a clean work surface, shape into a round, cover with clingfilm and chill in the freezer for 30 minutes.

Meanwhile, cure the rhubarb. Toss the rhubarb, salt, sugar, lemon thyme and fennel seeds together in a small bowl. Cover with a plate or tea towel and leave to cure at room temperature for 20 minutes. Drain the rhubarb in a colander, rinse and pat dry with a clean tea towel or kitchen paper. Leave in a cool place until ready to use.

Preheat the oven to 180°C/160°C fan/350°F/Gas 4.

Lightly grease a 23cm/9in fluted tart tin with butter. Remove the dough from the freezer and use the largest holes on a box grater to grate the dough into the centre of the tin in three stages. After each third, press the dough into the base and sides of the tin until they are completely covered to the top lip in an even layer. Prick the base of the pastry all over with a fork, then cover with baking

paper or foil, making sure some of the paper hangs over the side. Fill with baking beans and blind bake in the oven for 15 minutes. Remove the beans and paper and bake for another 12 minutes to cook the base until golden. Remove from the oven and leave to cool. Leave the oven on.

Meanwhile, for the filling, melt the butter in a large frying pan over a medium heat until melted and bubbling. Add the onions and a large pinch of salt. Fry, stirring frequently, for 8 minutes until the onions are soft and translucent. Reduce the heat to low and cook, stirring occasionally, for 25 minutes, or until the onions have reduced in volume by half and are golden and sweet. Remove from the heat.

Whisk the eggs, cream, parsley and mustard together in a medium bowl, then stir in the onions to combine. Pour the filling into the tart case and dot over the cured rhubarb. Crumble over the goat's cheese and scatter the lemon thyme over the top.

Bake the tart in the oven for 25 minutes, or until set. Leave to cool in the tin for 10 minutes before removing and slicing into wedges. Serve with a green salad and boiled new potatoes. The tart will keep covered in the fridge for up to three days. Reheat gently in a low oven before serving.

Creamy cauliflower pasta with cured egg yolks

Pasta blodfresych hufennog gyda melynwy hallt

Prep time: 25 minutes, plus 24 hours – 5 days curing
Cook time: 35 minutes

4

For the egg yolks
300g/10½oz finer flaked
   sea salt
75g/2¾oz caster sugar
2 rosemary sprigs, leaves picked and
   chopped
Finely grated zest of 1 unwaxed lemon
4 medium egg yolks

For the pangrattato
2 tbsp extra virgin olive oil
75g/2¾oz soft white breadcrumbs
½ tsp finer flaked sea salt
3 rosemary sprigs, leaves picked and
   finely chopped
1 garlic clove, finely chopped
Grated zest of ½ unwaxed lemon

For the pasta
1 cauliflower (about 500g/1lb 2oz), broken
   into florets, stalk roughly chopped
50g/1¾oz blanched almonds, roasted
   until golden brown
100ml/3½fl oz double cream
3 tbsp extra virgin olive oil
2 banana shallots, finely chopped
2 garlic cloves, finely sliced
3 anchovy fillets in oil
240g/8½oz penne or rigatoni pasta
¼ whole nutmeg, grated
1 small bunch of parsley, leaves picked
   and finely chopped
Grated zest of ½ unwaxed lemon
Finer flaked sea salt

Cured egg yolks are one of those magic things you can do in the kitchen – tucking them away in the fridge to transform. You can make them 24 hours in advance for a soft-centred yolk, as we have here, or five days in advance for a yolk that can be grated, not unlike bottarga (any leftovers can be grated over the buttermilk dressed salad on p.22, grilled asparagus or a spring risotto). The pasta is topped with pangrattato, a 'poor-man's Parmesan' from Italy, which is rich in both flavour and texture.

For the egg yolks, mix the salt, sugar, chopped rosemary and lemon zest together in a large bowl. Tip half of the mixture into a large container with a lid, then use a spoon to make four round wells in the curing mixture, about the size of the yolks, leaving at least 2cm/¾in space between each well. Lower the egg yolks into the wells and cover with the remaining salt mixture. Cover with a lid and leave in the fridge to cure for 24 hours for a soft-centred yolk, or five days for a firmer, grateable yolk.

Next, make the pangrattato. Heat the oil in a small frying pan over a medium heat. When it shimmers, add the breadcrumbs, salt, rosemary and garlic and stir to combine. Cook, stirring frequently for 5–7 minutes until golden and crispy all over. Transfer to a bowl, add the lemon zest and stir to combine. When the pangrattato is cool, transfer to a bowl or container and cover with an airtight lid. Store for up to a week at room temperature.

When the egg yolk is cured to your liking, bring a large saucepan of water to the boil. Add a generous pinch of salt, then lower in the cauliflower and return to a rolling boil. Cook for 5–7 minutes until very tender to the point of a sharp knife. Remove from the heat and use a slotted spoon to transfer the cauliflower to a food processor with the almonds. Leave the water in the pan to cook the pasta. Pulse until the cauliflower is very finely chopped and resembles breadcrumbs. Pour the cream and 2 tablespoons of the oil into a jug. With the food processor motor running, slowly pour in the cream and oil mixture, removing the lid and scraping down the sides of the bowl occasionally until all the mixture is used up. Set aside.

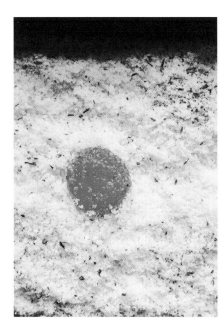

Heat the remaining oil in a small frying pan over a medium heat, add the shallots and a pinch of salt and fry, stirring frequently, for 3 minutes until the shallot is soft. Add the garlic and anchovies and press down with a wooden spoon on the anchovies to break them up. Stir for another 2 minutes, by which time, the anchovies should look like they are 'melted' and the garlic should be golden brown.

Return the pan of water to the boil and add another generous pinch of salt. Cook the pasta according to the packet instructions, then drain, reserving 125ml/4¼fl oz of the pasta cooking water. Return the pasta to the pan over a low heat. Pour in the shallot and anchovy mixture, the creamy cauliflower sauce, the reserved pasta water and grate over the nutmeg. Add the chopped parsley and stir until the thick sauce coats every piece of pasta. Cover with a lid and keep warm.

Remove the egg yolks from the fridge. Carefully lower into a bowl of cold water and rub away any salt that clings to the yolks. Each one should look like a glossy apricot. Pat dry before serving.

Spoon the pasta into warmed bowls and top with either a soft-centred egg yolk or grated egg yolk. Sprinkle a tablespoon of pangrattato over each bowl with the rest in a bowl on the table. Scatter with lemon zest and serve immediately.

Salt beef

We often make this recipe when we are expecting a houseful of guests. It's a perfect dish for entertaining at a weekend as it can be cured and cooked ahead, then eaten with hot or cold accompaniments as a main meal or a picnic. If eaten hot you can add creamy mashed potato and roast cabbage or serve in slices with pickles, and any leftovers can be used in place of pastrami in the Reuben Sandwich (p.121), or stuffed into homemade bagels or muffins. Don't let timings put you off, it's a surprisingly simple recipe and you will be highly rewarded by your forward planning.

1.5kg/3lb 4¾oz Welsh black beef brisket

1 garlic clove, peeled

6 juniper berries

1 tsp black peppercorns

6 fresh bay leaves

45g/1½oz finer flaked sea salt

20g/¾oz soft brown sugar

2 yellow onions, quartered

2 large carrots, cut into chunks

2 celery sticks, cut into 2cm/¾in pieces

½ head of garlic, sliced in
  half horizontally

🕐 2¾ hours – 3¾ hours, plus 7 days curing

🍴 Serves 6–8

Wash the beef and pat dry. Using a pestle and mortar, crush the garlic, juniper berries and peppercorns, then shred the bay leaves using a knife or your fingers and put them all into a medium bowl with the salt and sugar and mix together until combined. Rub the mixture all over the beef, then place the beef in a large ziplock bag. Leave in the fridge to cure for seven days, turning the beef over each day.

When the beef is ready, remove if from the bag and rinse thoroughly under cold running water. Discard the cure. Put the beef into a large saucepan of cold water and leave to soak somewhere cool overnight.

The next day, remove the beef from the pan and discard the water. Return the beef to the pan and cover in fresh, cold water. Add all the vegetables to the pan and bring to the boil. Reduce the heat to a low simmer, cover the pan with a tight-fitting lid and cook for 2½–3½ hours until the meat is meltingly tender. Check with a skewer if unsure. Serve the beef warm with a little of the broth spooned over. Alternatively, leave the meat to cool in the liquor and then store in the fridge in a covered dish. Eat within 3–4 days.

Halen Môn signature streaky bacon

Brithgig moch Halen Môn

🕐 15 minutes, plus 7 days curing

🍴 Makes approximately 30 rashers, depending on thickness

Bacon is fantastic. The combination of salt, sugar, aromatics and time transform a simple pork belly into the best start to the day. For those that enjoy the ritual of a carefully constructed bacon sandwich, this recipe may be the gateway into the world of curing, and it will certainly elevate any bacon sandwich to another level. It's also a process that can be done with children over the course of a week or so.

500g/1lb 2oz muscovado sugar
500g/1lb 2oz finer flaked sea salt
12 juniper berries
20 cracked black peppercorns
5 bay leaves, shredded (this can be combined or replaced with a similar amount of thyme, rosemary or sage depending on your preference)
2kg/4lb 6½oz piece pork belly, skin on
Malt vinegar, for wiping

Mix all the dry cure ingredients together in a large bowl until thoroughly combined.

Trim the pork belly into a piece of meat you can imagine slicing bacon from. Leave in the flat rib bones if they are present and leave the skin on. It doesn't need to be perfect – just tidy it up a little.

Put 20 per cent of the cure mix into a large non-metallic container (a fridge drawer works well or a large plastic container). Add the pork belly and using clean hands, rub the cure all over the pork, focusing on the flesh rather than the skin. Leave the pork belly, skin-side down, in the container covered with a tea towel for 24 hours in the bottom of the fridge. Put the unused dry cure into a large jar or airtight container for use later.

The next day, the pork belly will be sitting in a pool of liquid, so pour away the liquid and rinse the pork under cold running water to remove the cure and pat dry. Put the pork back into the container and add a large handful of the reserved dry cure. Using clean hands, rub the cure all over the pork, then leave, skin-side down, in the container covered with a tea towel in the fridge for another 24 hours. Rinse the pork and repeat this process each day for another three days. By this time you should have used all the dry cure. You will notice that less and less liquid is drawn from the belly each day and the meat will darken and firm up, as it is becoming bacon.

After five days of curing, remove the pork from the container and rinse it under cold running water. Pat dry with kitchen paper, then wipe the meat all over with a cloth soaked in malt vinegar. Wrap loosely in baking paper, then wrap in a tea towel and leave to dry in the fridge for another five days.

The bacon is now ready for cooking. Slice off as much bacon as you need. If you would like thick-cut bacon for sandwiches, then slice off strips about 3mm/^{1}/8in thick, or if you want to go for a bacon steak, go up to 10mm/½in. After slicing, wrap the bacon in the paper and towel and return to fridge. It will remain happily back in the bottom of your fridge, wrapped in the paper and cloth for up to two months.

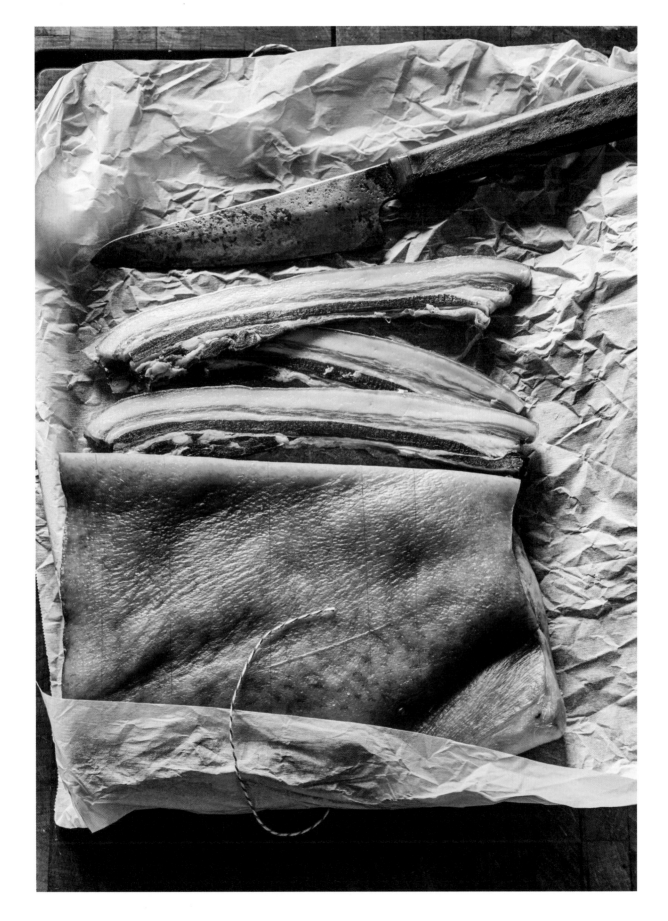

Roasted celeriac with peppercorn sauce

Celeriac rhost gyda saws pupur du

Prep time: 15 minutes,
plus 90 minutes curing
Cook time: 1 hour 10 minutes

4

This is a rich and delicious meal, with an outrageously good peppercorn sauce that vegetarians so often miss out on. Celeriac has seen a revival over the past year or two, and rightly so – it has a satisfying flavour and bite, only intensified by the curing process. Serve with good-quality chips and a green salad for a wonderful Sunday supper.

For the celeriac

1kg/2lb 3¼oz celeriac, scrubbed clean

100g/3½oz finer flaked sea salt

50g/1¾oz light soft brown sugar

1 tsp fennel seeds

¼ tsp ground black pepper

3 tbsp extra virgin olive oil

Chips (p.64), to serve

For the peppercorn sauce

50g/1¾oz butter

2 banana shallots, finely chopped

2 tbsp roughly crushed green peppercorns

1 tsp black peppercorns

1 tsp dried tarragon

¼ tsp paprika

½ tsp Marmite

125ml/4¼fl oz brandy

90ml/3¼fl oz double cream

Finer flaked sea salt

Start by curing the celeriac. Line a large baking sheet with baking paper. Cut the celeriac in half from top to bottom. Lay one half flat on a chopping board and cut the knobbly root into four wedges. Lay the wedges on the lined tray and repeat with the other celeriac half. You should have eight roughly even-sized wedges.

Mix the remaining ingredients, except the oil, together in a small bowl to combine, then scatter the mixture over the celeriac, evenly covering each piece. Cover the baking sheet with a clean tea towel and leave to cure for 1½ hours at room temperature, by which time some liquid drawn out from the celeriac will have mixed with the dry curing mixture.

Preheat the oven to 200°C/180°C fan/400°F/Gas 6.

Rinse the celeriac under cold running water and pat dry. Discard the curing mixture, then arrange the celeriac on a large baking sheet. Pour over the oil and toss the celeriac to evenly coat it. There is no need to season the celeriac as the cure will have worked its way into the centre of the wedges. Making sure the celeriac is in an even layer on the baking sheet, roast in the oven for 20 minutes. Turn the celeriac wedges over and return to the oven for another 25–30 minutes until they are caramelised in places and completely tender to the point of a knife. Keep warm while you make the peppercorn sauce.

Melt the butter in a small saucepan over a medium heat until melted and it begins to sizzle. Add the shallots and ½ teaspoon salt and fry, stirring occasionally, for 5 minutes, or until soft and translucent. Stir in the peppercorns and toast for 2 minutes until fragrant. Add the tarragon, paprika and Marmite and stir to combine before pouring in the brandy. Bring to a simmer and cook until the liquid has reduced by a third. Pour in 75ml/2½fl oz water and bring to a simmer again. Cook gently for 5 minutes, then pour in the cream and cook for 4–5 minutes over a low heat so the sauce is simmering gently but not steaming. When the sauce has thickened to a double cream consistency, remove from the heat. Taste and add a pinch more salt if you like, although it may not need seasoning as the sauce was seasoned from the outset with the shallots.

Serve a couple of celeriac wedges per person accompanied by the chips with the peppercorn sauce in a warm jug for pouring over.

Mackerel with fennel + rhubarb

Macrell gyda ffenigl a riwbob

🕐 1 hour, plus 1–4 hours curing
and pickling

🍴 4

At the height of summer, it's
rare to find a rocky outcrop on
Anglesey without a fisherman
setting up camp, patiently waiting
for mackerel. This dish is all about
the combination of textures and
strong flavours; the fattiness from
the cured fish pairs so well with the
sharpness of the rhubarb, which in
turn contrasts with the sweetness
in the fennel. It's a sophisticated
starter that is much greater than
the sum of its parts.

4 mackerel fillets (ask your fishmonger
to de-bone them)
1 tbsp crushed celery salt
40g/1½oz) finer flaked sea salt
50g/1¾oz soft light brown sugar
4 dill sprigs, leaves picked, to serve

For the fennel + rhubarb

100g/3½oz rhubarb, cut into 2cm/¾in
pieces, plus 75g/2¾oz for pickling
1 fennel bulb (about 400g/14oz),
sliced lengthways through the root
into 5mm/¼in slices, plus 100g/3½oz
for pickling
Juice of ½ orange
½ tsp finer flaked sea salt, plus 1 tsp
for pickling
3 tbsp olive oil
1 round shallot or ½ banana shallot,
finely diced
50ml/1¾fl oz apple cider vinegar
2 tsp caster sugar
Freshly ground black pepper

Start by curing the mackerel. Pat the fillets dry and set aside. Mix
both salts and the sugar together in a small bowl until combined,
then spread a third of the mixture over the base of a container
just large enough to hold the mackerel fillets in a single layer. Lay
the mackerel, skin-side down, in the cure mix and top with the
remaining mixture so that each fillet is evenly coated. Cover with
a clean tea towel and leave to cure in the fridge for 1 hour.

Remove the mackerel from the fridge and rinse off the cure. Pat
dry again and return to the fridge to continue drying in a cold
environment while you prepare the vegetables.

Preheat the oven to 180°C/160°C fan/350°F/Gas 4. Grease a
large roasting tray.

Toss the 100g/3½oz rhubarb pieces and 400g/14oz fennel slices
in the prepared roasting tray with the orange juice, salt and
enough oil to coat. Season with pepper, then roast in the oven for
15–20 minutes until tender; you want them to keep their shape
and texture.

Meanwhile, chop the remaining fennel and rhubarb finely into
5mm/¼in cubes, then add to a medium bowl with the shallot,
vinegar, sugar and 50ml/1¾fl oz water and mix to combine. If
the vegetables aren't submerged in the liquid, top up with equal
quantities of vinegar and water until they are covered. Cover with
a plate or tea towel and leave to pickle for at least 20 minutes or up
to 4 hours, depending on how strong you like your pickle to taste,
as the flavour intensifies over time.

Use a sharp knife to cut the mackerel fillets in half lengthways.
Carefully make a slice between the skin and the flesh and, using
the knife to hold the flesh down on a chopping board, pull the skin
away and discard. Cut the cured mackerel into 2cm/¾in pieces
and arrange the mackerel between four plates. Divide the roasted
vegetables between the plates (they can be served warm or at
room temperature) and top each of the mackerel pieces with a
¼ teaspoon of the pickled vegetables. Any extra pickled rhubarb
mixture can be covered and kept in the fridge to serve with roasted
goat's cheese, smoked salmon, or roast pork. Scatter over the dill
leaves and serve immediately.

Whisky cured hot-smoked salmon

Eog mŵg poeth wedi'i halltu â wisgi

15–45 minutes, plus 6 hours curing

Makes 4 fillets

Hot smoking isn't an exact science and it largely depends on your equipment, but the results are definitely worth the effort. We like to smoke over oak wood chips as they give such an incredible natural flavour. If you don't own a hot smoker, you can buy small, inexpensive wood chip smoker boxes that sit in the embers of the barbecue that work well. You can also try experimenting with other ingredients, such hot-smoked halloumi or tomatoes on the vine – they are delicious. You will also need a foil tray, or you can make one with layers of foil and some oak wood chips for this recipe.

4 salmon fillets, about 125g/4½oz each
50g/1¾oz honey
100g/3½oz caster sugar
100g/3½oz finer flaked sea salt
40g/1½oz smoked sea salt
50ml/1¾fl oz whisky
8 juniper berries
Extra virgin olive oil, for brushing

Pat the salmon fillets dry. Mix the honey, sugar, both salts, whisky and juniper berries together in a small bowl until evenly combined. Open a large, sealable plastic bag and spread a third of the whisky cure on the bottom, then place the salmon fillets on the cure, skin-side down. Use a spoon to spread the remaining cure over the top and sides of the fillets until it is all used. Close the bag and roll it up from the sealed side to tightly contain the salmon. Place the bag in a tray and top with a plate or board to weigh it down. Leave to cure in the fridge for 6 hours.

After the curing time, rinse the salmon under cold running water to remove the salty cure. The salmon should feel firmer and have turned a brighter shade of pink. Pat the fillets dry and brush all over with olive oil.

Prepare your smoking equipment. If smoking over a barbecue, prepare a disposable aluminium tray by poking holes in the tray all around with a metal skewer. Brush the salmon with olive oil (this helps the smoke flavour to 'stick') and place in the tray, and cover tightly with foil. Place a smoker box filled with wood chips on the red embers of the barbecue and, when smoke starts to emit from the holes, place the tray on the grill to hot smoke the salmon. This could take anywhere from 10–40 minutes, depending on the heat of the embers and the proximity of the salmon to the heat. Alternatively, use a hot smoker following the manufacturer's instructions. Whatever method you choose, keep a close eye on the salmon while it's smoking.

Test the salmon for doneness by checking the thickest part of the fillet; if it flakes easily, has firm flesh and is a uniform paler pink colour, it is done. If the cooking time is taking too long, or the heat is uneven (unfortunately a risk for home-made barbecues), the fillets can be finished in an oven preheated to 200°C/180°C fan/400°F/Gas 6 for a few minutes.

Serve the salmon warm or cool. Alternatively, put the salmon into an airtight container and store in the fridge for up to five days before eating.

Ideas for serving:

• Flake the fillets and mix with new potatoes, herbs and lettuce for a flavourful salad.

• Gently mix the fillets with a little lemon juice and finely diced shallot in a bowl to make rillettes to serve on crackers with chives.

• Flake the fillets and stir through cooked spaghetti with rocket and chilli.

• Serve with lemon wedges, soft cheese and bagels.

Fresh corn polenta with slow-roasted tomatoes + peppers

Polenta grawn ffres gyda thomatos a phupurau rhost

🕐 Prep time: 20 minutes, plus 30 minutes curing
Cook time: 1 ½ hours

🍴 4

For the oven dried tomatoes + peppers

4 red romano peppers, cut into 6 strips lengthways (seeds and stalk discarded)

500g/1lb 2oz cherry tomatoes, halved

1½ tbsp finer flaked sea salt

1 tsp caster sugar

⅛ tsp freshly ground black pepper

2 garlic cloves, crushed

½ tsp dried tarragon

3 tbsp extra virgin olive oil

2 tsp sherry vinegar

Finely grated zest of 1 unwaxed lemon

1 tbsp lemon juice

1 tsp honey

Handful of basil leaves

For the polenta

6 corn on the cobs

2 tbsp extra virgin olive oil

15g/½oz butter

1 onion, finely sliced

1 tsp finer flaked sea salt

2 garlic cloves, finely sliced

2 bay leaves

550ml/18½fl oz vegetable stock

30g/1oz Parmesan cheese, grated

Finer flaked sea salt and freshly ground black pepper

Some dream of polenta and its uniformly wonderful texture, while others write it off as boring, but this is a rare recipe that pleases most people. The comfort of the fresh polenta is topped off by cured and oven-dried tomatoes and peppers, which you will want to snack on straight from the tray. If you've never made it before, fresh corn polenta has a very different texture to the ground cornmeal polenta that you buy in the shops – it has a bit more bite but every bit as comforting.

Arrange the peppers and tomatoes in a large roasting tray. Mix the salt, sugar, pepper, garlic and tarragon together in a small bowl until combined, then scatter over the vegetables in the tray and use clean hands to toss everything together. Leave to cure at room temperature for 30 minutes.

Preheat the oven to 150°C/130°C fan/300°F/Gas 2.

After the curing time, place the vegetables to oven-dry on the middle shelf of the oven for 1½ hours. Open the oven door every 30 minutes to release the steam and help the flavour to concentrate as the vegetables cook.

Meanwhile, mix the oil, vinegar, lemon zest, juice and honey together in a large bowl (the vegetables will be added later, so you will want ample space to dress them) and set the bowl aside.

Meanwhile, prepare the corn for the polenta. Hold a corncob (stripping away any papery leaves or fibres) in the centre of a wide bowl and use a serrated knife to saw down the sides of the cob to release the kernels, turning as you go. Use the centre of the cob for vegetable stock and repeat with the remaining corncobs until all the kernels are in the bowl. Set aside.

Heat the oil and butter in a large saucepan over a medium heat until the butter is melted and bubbling. Add the onion and salt and cook over a medium heat, stirring occasionally, for 8 minutes, or until the onion is soft and translucent. Add the garlic and bay leaves and cook for another minute until fragrant. Stir in the sweetcorn kernels and cook for 2 minutes before pouring in the stock. Bring the mixture to the boil, then reduce the heat to a simmer and cook gently for 20 minutes, or until the sweetcorn is tender.

Remove the pan from the heat and use a stick blender to blitz the mixture until smooth, taking care as it may still be hot and spit (alternatively, use a jug blender and return to the pan after blending). Stir in the Parmesan. Season generously with black pepper, taste and add salt if you like, remembering that the vegetables are very well-seasoned and the contrast of sweetcorn and intensely flavoured vegetables is what you are aiming for.

Remove the vegetables from the oven and toss in the dressing. Add all but a few of the basil leaves and toss again. Divide the polenta between warmed bowls and top with the vegetables. Scatter over the reserved basil and serve immediately.

Both the polenta and vegetables (without the dressing and herbs) can be made up to three days in advance, covered and stored in the fridge. Reheat the polenta and vegetables gently before serving.

Lemony courgette tempura

Tempura corbwmpen a lemon

Prep time: 10 minutes,
plus 20 minutes curing
Cook time: 15 – 20 minutes

4 as a starter

Tempura is a dish all about texture, and curing the courgette here gives the ultimate pillowy contrast to the wonderfully satisfying crunch of the exterior batter. Finish with a few flakes of sea salt and bob really is your uncle. Two things will ensure your batter is a success: making sure the water is very cold and mixing it all together at the last minute to ensure lots of light bubbles.

25g/1oz finer flaked sea salt

1½ tsp caster sugar

Grated zest of 1 unwaxed lemon

10 lemon thyme sprigs

2 courgettes (about 350g/12¼oz prepared weight), cut into 10cm/4in batons

400ml/14fl oz vegetable oil, for deep-frying

110g/3¾oz plain flour

40g/1½oz cornflour

200ml/7fl oz ice-cold sparkling water

Lemon wedges, to serve

Mix the salt, sugar and lemon zest together in a large bowl. Pick the leaves from two sprigs of thyme, reserving the rest for later and mix into the salt and sugar mixture. Toss the courgettes in the lemon salt mix so that each piece of courgette is evenly coated and set aside to cure for 20 minutes, but no longer as the courgettes will become too salty.

Meanwhile, line a baking sheet with kitchen paper. Pour the oil for deep-frying into a medium saucepan, so it comes at least 4cm/1½in up the side. Clip on a sugar thermometer and set aside. Divide the flour between one large and one small bowl, with 60g/2¼oz in the larger bowl and 50g/1¾oz in the smaller one. Add the cornflour to the larger bowl.

Rinse the courgettes in a colander under cold running water for at least 90 seconds to wash away the salt. Toss with your hands while you rinse, to ensure every piece is exposed to the water. Pat dry.

Heat the oil for deep-frying over a medium-high heat while you prepare the batter.

Pour the sparkling water into the large bowl containing the cornflour and plain flour and mix gently to combine for 20 seconds. Don't overmix or worry about making sure the batter is completely smooth. A few lumps here and there are fine, but the batter should resemble the consistency of single cream.

When the oil reaches 185°C/365°F on the thermometer, dip the courgettes into the small bowl of flour to coat on both sides, then dip the coated slices into the batter and carefully lower into the hot oil. Deep-fry in small batches for 2 minutes on each side until light golden and crispy. Use a slotted spoon to turn the courgettes and lift them out onto the lined baking sheet to drain away excess oil.

Finally, dip the remaining lemon thyme stalks into the batter and carefully drop into the hot oil to deep-fry for 30 seconds. Drain on the paper with the courgettes.

Serve immediately in a warmed serving dish with lemon wedges for squeezing over.

Root vegetable + blood orange salad

Salad llysiau'r pridd ac oren coch

Prep time: 20 minutes, plus
40 minutes curing
Cook time: 45 minutes

4

Curing root vegetables serves to temper their earthiness and amplify their jammy, savoury character to a deliciously noticeable degree. We like to use blood oranges in this salad, but if they are not in season then try navel oranges.

500g/1lb 2oz beetroot, peeled and cut
    into 2cm/¾in wedges
250g/9oz parsnips, peeled and cut into
    3cm/1¼in pieces
250g/9oz celeriac, peeled and cut into
    3cm/1¼in pieces
90g/3¼oz finer flaked sea salt
75g/2¾oz caster sugar
1 garlic clove, grated
Grated zest of 1 unwaxed blood orange
½ tsp cumin seeds
¼ tsp ground black pepper
Olive oil, for drizzling
100g/3½oz goat's cheese log
1 tbsp honey
2 blood oranges
250g/9oz pouch cooked Puy lentils
Juice of ½ lemon
1 head red endive, leaves separated
50g/1¾oz hazelnuts, toasted and
    roughly chopped
3 parsley sprigs, leaves picked
3 tarragon sprigs, leaves picked
2 tbsp extra virgin olive oil
Freshly ground black pepper

Arrange the beetroot on a roasting tray in an even layer and the parsnips and celeriac on another. Rub the salt and sugar together with the garlic clove, orange zest, cumin and pepper in a small bowl to combine. Divide the salt and sugar mixture between the vegetables in the two trays and toss to coat every piece in the cure. Leave to cure at room temperature for 40 minutes (but no longer as the vegetables will become too salty).

Preheat the oven to 200°C/180°C fan/400°F/Gas 6.

Keeping the beetroot separate from the other vegetables, rinse them all thoroughly under cold running water and pat dry. Rinse the trays to wash away the cure and dry them. Put the beetroot onto one tray and the parsnips and celeriac on another. Drizzle the vegetables with enough olive oil to coat in a thin layer and roast in the oven for 35–40 minutes until tender and caramelised in places. About 15 minutes before the end of the cooking time, remove the beetroot tray from the oven and put the goat's cheese on top of the beetroot. Drizzle the honey over the cheese and return the tray to the oven.

Meanwhile, slice the top and bottom off the blood oranges and use a serrated knife to cut away the skin and pith. Cut the blood oranges into 1cm/½in rounds, discarding any pips. Set the slices aside until ready to use. Warm the lentils through in a large frying pan, then remove from the heat and dress with 1 tablespoon of olive oil and the lemon juice.

Remove the roasted vegetables from the oven and while the cheese is still warm, roughly break it up with a fork into wobbly chunks. Stir the lentils through the vegetables and cheese.

Arrange the roasted vegetable mixture on a serving platter. Break the blood orange slices into smaller pieces and tuck among the vegetables along with the endive leaves. Scatter over the hazelnuts and herbs and drizzle with the extra virgin olive oil. Season with black pepper and serve immediately.

Dill + beetroot trout gravadlax

Gravadlax brithyll gyda betys a dil

Trout is an expensive fish, so if you're splashing out, you may as well choose a recipe that takes time and care but gives you an impressive result. Beetroot brings both colour and flavour to this beautiful fish, and the mustard sauce takes it to a whole new level. Try the mustard sauce with the Whisky-cured Hot-smoked Salmon on p.142, or even on hot new potatoes. Traditionally, gravadlax is made with salmon in Nordic countries for celebrations and special occasions, but we like the slightly lighter flavour of trout.

For the gravadlax

1 x 700g/25oz side of trout, filleted and pin bones removed

110g/3¾oz caster sugar

75g/2¾oz flaked sea salt

¼ tsp ground black pepper

65ml/2¼fl oz gin

50g/1¾oz dill, roughly chopped, plus extra sprigs, leaves picked, to garnish

400g/14oz beetroot, washed with the tough bits of rind cut off, grated

For the mustard sauce

1 tbsp Dijon mustard

1 tbsp wholegrain mustard

1 tbsp soft light brown sugar

1 tbsp lemon juice

1 tbsp apple cider vinegar

2 tbsp rapeseed oil

3 dill sprigs, leaves picked and finely chopped

 20 minutes, plus 48 hours curing

12

Pat the trout dry all over, then set aside. Mix the sugar, salt, pepper and gin together in a small bowl. Using a large, sealable plastic bag, or clingfilm, spread a third of the cure over the base. Place the trout, skin-side down, on the cure and use a spoon and spatula to spread the remaining cure over the top and sides of the fish. Scatter the dill evenly over the fish and top with the beetroot to cover (you should have plenty of bright purple beetroot to completely cover the fish). Seal the plastic bag or wrap the fish tightly in the clingfilm to seal. Place the trout in a tray in which it fits snugly and cover with a board or tray that fits inside. Place a couple of jars on top of the board to weigh it down. Leave to cure in the fridge for 48 hours, turning the fish twice during this time, keeping it covered and weighed down with the board and jars in between.

Remove the trout from the fridge and unwrap it. Scrape away the beetroot and dill and discard, then cut off a thin slice of fish to taste. If you prefer (i.e. if the taste of the cure is too strong for you), rinse it gently under cold running water to wash away any excess cure. Using a sharp knife, slice the fish into long, thin slices, avoiding the skin, and set the sliced fish aside.

Whisk all the ingredients for the sauce together in a small bowl until a thick, emulsified sauce forms. Transfer to a serving bowl.

Arrange the slices of cured trout on a platter with toasted rye bread or oatcakes alongside. Serve a slice of the cured fish on the bread or oatcakes and drizzle with a little of the mustard sauce. Top with dill. After removing the cure, (assuming the trout hasn't been kept at room temperature for longer than an hour), it can be kept covered in the fridge for up to three days.

Tofu with minty peas + pickles

Tofu gyda phys mintys a phiclau

In Japan, tofu makers and salt makers have a special relationship. Nigari, a natural mineral byproduct of sea salt production, is an ingredient essential in traditional Japanese tofu making, so you will usually find the factories near to each other. Curing the tofu in this recipe with a salt and sugar mix seasons it beautifully before you begin cooking. This makes an excellent lunch if you put it into a wrap with some mayonnaise.

For the pickled vegetables

1 large red onion, finely sliced into rounds

20 radishes, finely sliced

6 tbsp apple cider vinegar

2 tsp caster sugar

Finer flaked sea salt

For the tofu

2 x 280g/10oz blocks firm tofu

4 tbsp finer flaked sea salt

2 tbsp soft light brown sugar

2 tsp sweet smoked paprika

1 tsp ground allspice

½ tsp ground ginger

6 tbsp rapeseed oil

1 lemon, cut into wedges, to serve (optional)

For the peas

500g/1lb 2oz frozen peas

4 tbsp extra virgin olive oil

2 garlic cloves, peeled and roughly chopped

Grated zest and juice of 1 unwaxed lemon

1 small bunch of mint, leaves picked

Freshly ground black pepper

Prep time: 10 minutes, plus 45 minutes curing and pickling
Cook time: 20 minutes

4

Start by pickling the vegetables. Put the red onion, radishes and vinegar into a medium bowl and, using clean hands, scrunch for 10 seconds. Add the sugar and ½ teaspoon salt and scrunch for another 30 seconds until you feel the vegetables soften. Cover the vegetables with a clean bowl that will nestle inside the mixing bowl and weigh down with a jar. Set aside while you prepare the rest.

Cut each block of tofu into six 1cm/½in slices and pat dry with a clean tea towel. Lay the slices flat on a plate so there is no overlap. Mix the salt, sugar and spices together in a small bowl, then scatter half over one side of the tofu, before turning the slices over and repeating with the other half of the mixture. You may need to dip the tofu into the curing mixture on the plate to ensure as much of the surface is covered as possible. Leave to cure for 45 minutes at room temperature.

Meanwhile, prepare the peas. Bring a small saucepan of water to the boil and add a large pinch of salt. Add the peas and return to the boil. Cook for 3 minutes, or until all the peas have risen to the surface and are tender. Drain and tip the peas into a food processor with the extra virgin olive oil, garlic, lemon zest and juice and the mint and blitz until a rough mash forms. Taste and add more salt and pepper according to your preference. Transfer to a heat-proof bowl, cover and keep warm in a low oven while you cook the tofu.

Rinse the tofu under cold running water and pat dry. Line a large plate with kitchen paper. Heat the rapeseed oil in a frying pan large enough to hold all the tofu slices over a medium heat. Add the tofu and fry for 3–4 minutes on each side until crisp and golden. Transfer to the lined plate with a spatula to drain off the excess oil.

Divide the pea mixture between four warmed plates and top with three slices of tofu. Drain the pickled vegetables and spoon 2 teaspoons of the vegetables over the tofu with the rest in a bowl on the table. Serve immediately with lemon wedges, if liked, alongside new potatoes or roasted root vegetables.

FLAVOURS
OF THE SEA

BLASAU'R MÔR

Proper potted shrimps

Berdys mewn menyn

Many fishmongers will sell potted shrimps but as with most edible things, it's well worth making your own – particularly for something as simple as this. Brown shrimps are sold cooked and peeled from most fishmongers and in larger supermarkets, but search for sustainably fished British brown shrimps, as they are smaller and tastier than warm water farmed ones. Traditionally, the shrimps are served spread over hot toast, allowing the clarified butter to soften and melt slightly, but it's also delicious served warmed and spooned over toasted bread or slices of thin Melba toast. If you prefer to serve the shrimps warm, rather than potted, stir them into the spiced butter rather than placing them in ramekins, and heat through over a low heat.

For the shrimps

250g/9oz butter

2 fresh bay leaves

½ tsp ground mace

⅛ tsp ground cayenne

200g/7oz cooked and peeled brown shrimps

Finer flaked sea salt and freshly ground black pepper

Lemon wedges, to serve

For the pickled shallot

1 banana shallot, cut into 2.5mm/⅛in rounds

1 tbsp apple cider vinegar

1 tsp caster sugar

Juice of ½ lemon

⅛ tsp finer flaked sea salt

🕐 20–30 minutes, plus 2 hours setting

🍴 4

Put the butter into a medium saucepan (try to avoid any non-stick saucepans for this as the black lining can make it hard to keep an eye on the butter) and melt over a medium-low heat. When all the butter is melted, control the temperature so that the butter is simmering slightly and watch it like a hawk for 7–8 minutes until the first golden flecks appear on the base of the pan. During this time, the milk solids should move from the surface of the butter to the base of the pan. Tilt and swirl the pan to check the colour of the solids (which will form the flecks that darken). Remove from the heat and pour the butter through a muslin cloth into a jug.

Wipe out the pan and pour two-thirds of the strained butter into it together with the bay leaves, mace, cayenne and a pinch of salt and black pepper. Bring to a simmer and simmer gently for 1 minute before removing from the heat and discarding the bay leaves.

Pat the shrimps dry and divide evenly between four ramekins. Use the back of a spoon to gently pack them into the ramekins. Pour over the spiced butter and leave to cool for about 20 minutes to room temperature before transferring them to the fridge to set for about 45 minutes. When set, pour over the remaining clarified butter and return to the fridge for 1 hour, or until completely set.

Meanwhile, prepare the pickled shallot. Put the shallot and all the remaining pickling ingredients into a small bowl and, using clean hands, scrunch the shallot until you feel the shallot start to soften. Weigh the shallot down by placing a clean bowl over the top and leave to pickle for at least 30 minutes or up to 2 hours.

Serve the shrimps spread over hot toast with lemon wedges for squeezing over and the pickled shallots alongside.

Grilled oysters in smoky spiced garlic butter

Wystrys wedi'u grilio mewn menyn mŵg sbeislyd

🕐 25 minutes

🍴 4 as a starter

Menai oysters are grown right in front of our Saltcote at Halen Môn – the raw seawater is an incredible resource. You can do the prep earlier then it's quick, easy (and impressive) to cook and serve. Your guests will automatically gravitate towards the chef and are almost guaranteed to impatiently burn themselves on the hot shells and molten butter, so please be careful! The hardest part of this dish is to find something to serve the oysters on. Rock oysters have an irregular cupped shell and when they come off the barbecue, they will be scalding hot and filled with bubbling butter. We have found the best thing is an old griddle pan but we have also used seaweed (when feeling fancy), pebbles or egg boxes (when desperate).

75g/2¾oz butter, softened

50g/1¾oz Parmesan cheese, finely grated

4 garlic cloves, finely grated

Finely grated zest and juice of ½ lemon

1 tsp hot smoked paprika, plus extra for dusting

1 tsp cayenne pepper

¼ tsp smoked sea salt

¼ tsp hot sauce

12 rock oysters

Small bunch of parsley, leaves picked and chopped

Lemon wedges, to serve

Mix the softened butter, cheese, garlic, lemon zest and juice, paprika, cayenne, salt and hot sauce together in a large bowl. Use a fork to work it into a smooth mixture. Empty the bowl onto a piece of clingfilm, big enough to hold the butter, then roll it into an even sausage shape about 2cm/¾in thick. Chill until ready for cooking.

Opening oysters can be tricky – even trickier after a few drinks by the barbecue with lots of people watching you, so open the oysters just before your guests arrive and make sure the oyster is completely detached from the shell to help with eating later. If you have not done this before, ask your fishmonger to show you (and refresh your memory with tutorials available online once you get home). You will need an oyster knife to do this at home.

Remove the grill from the barbecue and light. Get your charcoal to the point where you cannot hold your hand over the heat for more than 10 seconds. Place the shucked oysters, cup-shell down, on the cold grill. You need to be careful to get them to remain upright so they don't spill their contents and add a 1cm/½in disc of the flavoured butter to each oyster. Very carefully lower the laden grill on to the barbecue. Depending on the heat, it will take 3–6 minutes before the butter is bubbling and this means the oyster is poached to perfection. Using tongs, move each oyster to a serving platter. Sprinkle with parsley and a dusting of paprika and serve with lemon wedges and crusty bread.

Note
The oysters can be cooked under a preheated hot grill if you don't want to light the barbecue; the cook time will be the same.

Samphire eggs hollandaise + English muffins

Hollandaise wyau llyrlys a myffins Seisnig

🕐 1 hour 15 minutes, plus 1½–2 hours rising

🍴 4

For the English muffins

350g/12¼oz strong white bread flour,
    plus extra for dusting

7g/¼oz fast-action dried yeast

7g/¼oz finer flaked sea salt

10g/¼oz caster sugar

50g/1¾oz butter, melted and cooled

1 medium egg, lightly beaten

215ml/7¼fl oz whole milk (or up to
    30ml/1fl oz more if the dough feels dry)

Vegetable oil, for oiling

Semolina or polenta, for dusting

Freshly ground black pepper

For the hollandaise

2 egg yolks

¼ tsp Dijon mustard

1 tsp white wine vinegar or up to 1 tbsp
    fresh lemon juice

155g/5¼oz butter

Squeeze of lemon juice

To serve

250g/9oz samphire, tough ends cut off
    and stalks broken into even-sized spears

1 tbsp white wine vinegar

1–2 eggs per person

Samphire has vibrant green stalks, a beautifully crisp texture and a saltiness that goes very well with eggs. It grows in summer abundance at Halen Môn, but is also available in fishmongers and many supermarkets, too. If you are gathering it yourself, wash very thoroughly before eating! Although relatively simple, this dish has lots of elements, so it's worth reading the recipe through before you begin. The hollandaise can be tricky splitting into scrambled eggs and butter if the water is too hot or you try to whisk in the butter too quickly but by adding a pinch of cornflour to the egg yolks you are more likely to succeed.

To make the English muffins, mix the flour, yeast, salt and sugar together in a large bowl until combined. Make a well in the centre and pour in the melted butter, egg and milk, then use a wooden spoon to mix the wet ingredients into the dry until a rough dough forms. Transfer the mixture to a lightly floured work surface and knead for 8–10 minutes until the dough is smooth and elastic. Lightly oil another large bowl and put the dough into it. Cover with a clean tea towel and leave to rise at room temperature for 1–1½ hours until the dough has risen and doubled in size.

Lightly dust a clean work surface with semolina and flour and place the dough in the centre. Dust a rolling pin with flour and roll the dough out until it is 2cm/¾in thick. Dust a large baking sheet with semolina and flour and set aside.

Using a 9cm/3½in ring cutter, cut out eight rounds from the dough, bringing it back together and rolling it out again until all the dough is used up. Transfer to the prepared baking sheet, cover with a tea towel and leave to prove at room temperature for another 30 minutes.

Heat a large, non-stick, lidded frying pan over a medium-low heat. Arrange 3–4 muffins in the pan and cover with a lid. Cook for 5–7 minutes on each side until puffed up and browned. Transfer to a wire rack and repeat with the remaining muffins until they are all cooked.

Leave the muffins to cool on the wire rack. Once cool, the muffins can be frozen in an airtight container for up to three months.

Next, make the hollandaise. Place the egg yolks in a heatproof bowl and, using a balloon whisk, whisk in the mustard and vinegar. Melt the butter gently in a saucepan until it just starts to bubble, then remove from the heat and transfer to a jug. Whisking constantly, slowly pour the butter into the egg yolk mixture in a thin, steady stream until all the butter is incorporated and the mixture is thick and glossy. Half-fill a saucepan with water and place over a medium heat until it comes to a simmer. Reduce the heat until the water is barely simmering, but still steaming, then set the yolk mixture over the pan of barely simmering water, making sure the base of the bowl doesn't touch the water and cook, stirring constantly, for 5–7 minutes until the sauce has thickened to the consistency of custard. Taste and add a squeeze of lemon juice and black pepper (remembering the samphire will be salty). Pour the hollandaise into a warmed serving jug, cover and keep warm while you cook the samphire and eggs.

Bring a pan of water to the boil, add the samphire and boil for 4 minutes, or until tender. Drain and set aside.

Line a plate with kitchen paper. Reduce the water in the pan to a gentle simmer, then use a wooden spoon to stir the water in a circular motion to create a whirlpool in the water. Pour in the vinegar, then crack in the eggs, two at a time, and simmer gently for 4 minutes, or until the whites are cooked and the outside of the yolks are just set. Using a slotted spoon, transfer the eggs to the lined plate to drain.

Use a serrated knife to cut the muffins in half, toasting each half if you prefer, before topping with one or two poached eggs, a quarter of the samphire and a generous spoon of the warm hollandaise. Season with black pepper and serve.

Herb-crusted salt marsh rack of lamb

Rac cig oen morfa mewn crwst perlysiau

🕐 30 minutes

🍴 4

Now for something a bit fancy. Rack of lamb is the prime cut of lamb and salt marsh lamb is the pinnacle of lamb – a sweet savoury meat that is revered in France (*l'agneau pré-salé*) and is only recently gaining the recognition that it deserves in the UK. Available from June to September, these animals move directly from their mother's milk to the coastal flora found on the estuary salt marshes. The result of this daily seasoning is a meat that is less fatty, more tender and sweeter than any mountain lamb. This is one of our fail-safe recipes for a special occasion.

50g/1¾oz panko breadcrumbs

2 garlic cloves, crushed or grated

50g/1¾oz herbs (parsley, thyme and chives are perfect, maybe add a little rosemary, too), finely chopped

Finely grated zest of 1 lemon

4 anchovy fillets, finely chopped

1kg/2lb 3¼oz French trimmed rack of lamb, cut into 4 equal portions (usually between 3–5 ribs per portion)

2 tbsp Dijon mustard

Finer flaked sea salt and freshly ground black pepper

Preheat the oven to 190°C/170°C fan/375°F/Gas 5.

Mix the breadcrumbs, garlic, herbs, pepper, lemon zest and anchovies together in a large bowl. This can be done in a food processor to save time (and get bright green breadcrumbs).

Season the lamb portions on all sides with a sprinkle of salt and pepper. Heat an ovenproof frying pan over a medium-high heat and sear the lamb on all sides. As well as sealing the portions, now is the time to render any significant amounts of fat that can be left on the top of the cut by some butchers. Take your time. If the temperature is too hot, then the fat will burn. It is better to have a slightly lower temperature and to keep moving the meat around. You want to have crispy, golden brown meat with most of the fat cap rendered. This should take at 5–10 minutes.

Remove the meat from the pan and, using a pastry brush, brush the meat with the mustard, taking care to leave the bones free of mustard. Don't wash up the frying pan – you are going to need it again. Roll the portions in the breadcrumb mixture making sure to cover all sides of the meat.

Return the portions to the frying pan and put the pan into the oven to finish the cooking for 15 minutes. Test the temperature in the centre of the rack with a meat thermometer. You should be aiming for 50°C/122°F for rare. Rest the meat on a plate or board covered with foil for at least 5 minutes.

To serve, slice down between the bones and arrange on each serving plate. You should get beautiful pink meat surrounded by a bright green crust.

Serve with the Seaweed smoked new potatoes (recipe overleaf) for something special.

Seaweed smoked new potatoes

Tatws newydd drwy fŵg gwymon

🕐 50–100 minutes, plus 30 minutes drying

🍴 4–6

This is fun to make and so delicious that it makes a feast on its own. The potatoes take on a moreish, savoury note, which, with the lemon pepper butter, means it goes well with grilled fish as well. You will need a smoking box and a barbecue, or a hot smoker for this recipe. We also collect seaweed from our local beach, rinse it thoroughly in fresh water and hang it on the washing line for a few days to crisp up – a fun activity if there are kids about, too.

1kg/2lb 3¼oz new potatoes
60g/2¼oz dried seaweed,
   such as kombu or wakame
1 tbsp demerara sugar
Olive oil, for drizzling
50g/1¾oz butter, softened
1 garlic clove, grated
Finely grated zest of 1 lemon and
   juice of ½
Finer flaked sea salt
Smoked sea salt and freshly ground
   black pepper
Chopped herbs, such as parsley, mint,
   dill or chervil, to serve

For smoking
150g wood smoking chips

Bring a large saucepan of water to the boil, then add a generous amount of fine sea salt and carefully submerge the potatoes. Boil for 8 minutes, or until just tender. Drain in a colander and leave to steam-dry for at least 30 minutes. Pierce each potato with the end of a sharp skewer.

Meanwhile, light a barbecue or hot smoker. Mix the smoking chips with the seaweed and sugar to begin smoking (if using a barbecue, mix the smoking chips with the seaweed and sugar in a smoker box to sit on the coals, under the grill).

In a mixing bowl, toss the potatoes with enough olive oil to coat and season generously with smoked salt. Arrange the potatoes in the centre of a large piece of foil, then gather up and fold the sides to seal. Poke holes with a skewer all over the foil and place on the rack of the smoker or barbecue. Smoke for 30–90 minutes until the potatoes are completely tender and smoky. The length of the smoking time will depend on your equipment and heat source. Using a tea towel or oven gloves, unwrap the foil to test the potatoes occasionally for flavour and tenderness, before sealing the foil using the tea towel to protect your hands from the heat. If your potatoes are ready before you anticipate, they can be kept warm wrapped in foil in an oven preheated to 120°C/100°C fan/250°F/Gas 1.

Meanwhile, make the flavoured butter. Put the softened butter into a medium bowl with the garlic, half the lemon zest and all the juice. Season generously with black pepper (about 40–50 turns of the pepper mill should do it) and use a fork to mix everything together until evenly combined.

When the potatoes are done, unwrap the foil with a tea towel, transfer the potatoes to a warmed bowl using a serving spoon and dot over the flavoured butter. Sprinkle with chopped herbs and the remaining lemon zest just before serving. Any leftover potatoes are fantastic in Niçoise salads or fried into a hash with spring or summer vegetables.

A rustic seaside tart

Tarten lan môr y werin

 1 hour 35 minutes, plus 10 minutes chilling

4–6

For the pastry

250g/9oz plain flour, plus extra
  for dusting
Pinch of finer flaked sea salt
125g/4¼oz butter, chilled and diced,
  plus extra for greasing
30ml/1fl oz oak-smoked water
  or water
95ml/3¼fl oz ice-cold water

For the filling

4–5 rashers of streaky bacon, diced
A good knob of butter
2 good handfuls of sea beet or spinach,
  washed
3 whole medium eggs, plus 3 egg yolks
100ml/3½fl oz milk
200ml/7fl oz single cream
150g/5¼oz potato, cooked and cut into
  small cubes
100g/3½oz strong Cheddar, grated
Finer flaked sea salt and freshly ground
  black pepper

Sea beet is a hardy coastal wild vegetable, not unlike a more seasoned chard, that grows along the beaches of Anglesey and much of the UK coast. Tender young leaves are at their best in spring, but you can find it year round, often among sand dunes or on the edges of fields. Rinse it thoroughly and avoid any patches popular with dog walkers. If it's too much of a stretch, then spinach can be used instead. This flaky pastry is a winner – we use our oak smoked water to bring a deeply savoury flavour to the tart, but if you don't have any, use more water.

Grease a 23cm/9in loose-bottomed cake tin.

Mix the flour and salt together in a large bowl. Add the diced butter and toss it around to coat the butter with the flour.

Mix the smoked water and ice-cold water together, then gradually add to the flour mixture (you may not need all the liquid, as the dough should hold together but not be sticky), bringing it together until it forms a soft dough with visible chunks of butter.

Roll out the pastry on a floured work surface into a long rectangle, about 1cm/⅓in thick. Fold the top third of the pastry into the middle, then fold the opposite third over it to create three layers. Turn the pastry by a quarter and repeat the rolling and folding process. Wrap the pastry in clingfilm and chill in the fridge for 10 minutes.

Repeat the folding process once more, wrap and refrigerate again.

Preheat the oven to 220°C/200°C fan/425°F/Gas 7.

Roll out the pastry on a floured work suface until it is wider all the way round than the tart tin. Carefully lower the pastry inside and press it into the corners. It is worth saving a little chunk of pastry at this point in case there are any holes that need patching up later.

Prick the base all over with a fork. Line the pastry case with baking paper and fill with baking beans, then blind bake in the oven for 20 minutes. Remove the tin from the oven and reduce the oven temperature to 180°C/160°C fan/350°F/Gas 4. As this is a flaky pastry it will have puffed up a little. Remove the beans and paper and bake for another 15 minutes, or until the pastry is golden brown.

Meanwhile, prepare the filling. Melt the butter in a hot pan over a medium heat and fry the bacon until crispy. Remove from the pan and leave to drain on kitchen paper. Add the sea beet to the hot pan and cook until gently wilted. If you are using spinach you may need to squeeze out excess liquid. Once wilted, transfer to a large bowl, add the bacon and potatoes and mix together until combined.

Whisk the eggs, egg yolks, milk and cream together in a small bowl, then season well with salt and pepper.

Fill the blind-baked tart case with the sea beet, potato and bacon mixture and sprinkle over the grated cheese. Pour in the egg, milk and cream mixture until it reaches the top of the tin, then bake in the oven for about 45 minutes, or until the mixture is slightly wobbly but set. Leave to cool in the tin before serving.

Eclade des moules

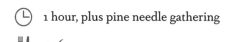

Eclade des moules originates from the Charente-Maritime region of France. Here, the pine forests run into the beautiful Ile de Ré beaches, which run into the Atlantic ocean. This is an identical set-up to one of our favourite nearby spots, Newborough beach, just down the road from Halen Môn. Added to that, the fact that Anglesey grows some of the best mussels around, makes it the perfect dish to eat on the salty island. This is a simple barbecue dish that is perfect to prepare in a large group. Everyone can help out in the assembly and the 'cooking' is spectacular. More than just being a piece of theatre, it also delivers a delicious way to enjoy mussels. The sweetness of the mussels is complemented by a smoky pine aroma. It doesn't take a genius to see why fisherman have been preparing mussels like this for years.

2kg/4lb 6½oz live mussels

A wooden board large enough to hold the mussels

A few nails and a hammer

Enough dry pine needles to cover mussels to a depth of about 15cm/6in (they need to be really, really dry, so if in doubt, collect them ahead of time and dry at home), a large bagful should do the trick

🕐 1 hour, plus pine needle gathering

🍴 4–6

As this dish need to be cooked outside, preferably on a beach, please make sure you are well away from any trees or anything that could be caught by the flames. Scrub the mussels under cold running water. Remove the beards and discard any mussels that are broken or don't close after a firm tap on a hard surface.

Lay your wooden board flat on the ground or on a stable platform. In the middle of the board, fix four nails in a square about 2.5cm/1in apart. Ask your helpers to arrange the mussels, hinge-side up until the entire board is covered or you have run out of mussels. Using the nails to support the first mussels, you will quickly be able to create concentric rings of mussels and it will end up looking like an art installation. If it doesn't and they keep falling over, put down your wine and use both hands! It's important that the mussels are arranged hinge-side up so that once they are cooked, the ash does not get into the flesh.

Once all the mussels are laid out, cover them with the dry pine needles, about 15cm/6in deep so they are completely covered. When you are ready, light the needles from a number of different points. They will take a short while to catch but when they do, they will burn ferociously, so do be careful and stand back. The intense heat will boil the seawater in the shells and steam the mussels. Let the pine needles burn out. it will usually take 5–6 minutes, then gently blow away the remaining ash. After a few minutes to let the shells cool, discard any mussels that haven't opened during cooking, then invite your guests forward to help themselves with their fingers.

Cold drinks and bread are all that's needed to accompany.

Note
This is as much a guide as a recipe and will feed four as a dramatic main course. To scale up to feed to an entire party allocate roughly 250g/9oz mussels per person for a starter or as part of a spread, and 500g/1lb 2oz per person if it's a main event.

Purple sprouting broccoli with anchovy

Brocoli coesog porffor gydag ansiofi

🕐 20 minutes

🍴 2 as a main when stirred through cooked pasta or grains

An absolute favourite in our garden, and in our kitchen, purple sprouting broccoli is delicious on its own, but this classic flavour pairing with anchovy somehow sharpens its rich, mineral character. Serve it on its own as an elegant starter or side, on toast for a simple lunch, or stirred through pasta or beans for a memorable supper. The anchovies act as the main seasoning here as their rich savouriness tastes more umami than fishy. Cut the tip of your chilli off and taste a tiny bit to judge how spicy it is before you decide how much to add.

350g/12¼oz purple sprouting broccoli, trimmed to even-sized pieces

50ml/1¾fl oz extra virgin olive oil

2 shallots, finely chopped

6 garlic cloves, finely sliced

1 large red chilli, finely sliced at an angle (you may need more or less according to the chilli heat and your taste)

6 anchovy fillets in oil

Finer flaked sea salt

Lemon wedges, to serve

Using a steamer basket suspended over a pan of boiling water on a high heat, steam the broccoli for 4 minutes until the stalks are just tender. Lift the steamer basket off the pan of water, and tip the broccoli into a colander suspended over the sink to steam-dry for about 15 minutes.

Heat the olive oil in a large frying pan over a medium heat. Add the shallots and a pinch of salt and fry for 3–4 minutes until just tender. Add the garlic, chilli and anchovies and use a wooden spoon to crush the anchovies until they melt into a paste. Stir to combine, controlling the heat so that the garlic turns golden but does not burn. Add the broccoli to the pan and stir through the anchovy-spiked oil until piping hot.

Transfer the broccoli to warmed plates, spooning the oil over every spear as you go. Serve with the lemon wedges for squeezing.

Charred cabbage wedges with seaweed butter

Darnau o fresych wedi'u golosgi gyda menyn gwymon

 30 minutes

4 as a side

If you have never charred cabbage before, you are in for a treat. Cooking it in this way makes for a far deeper, more satisfying flavour, only amplified by the umami of the seaweed. Serve alongside toad in the hole or with a hearty stew.

1 January King or Savoy cabbage, cut into quarters through the root

175g/6oz butter

1 tsp ground mace

2 tsp seaweed flakes, plus extra for sprinkling

1 tsp finer flaked sea salt

75ml/2½fl oz dry sherry, such as Fino or Manzanilla

Juice of 1 lemon

Preheat the oven to 120°C/100°C fan/250°F/Gas 1.

Heat a large deep sauté pan over a high heat, place the cabbage wedges in the pan with one of the cut-sides facing down, pour in 150ml/5fl oz water and cover with a lid or foil. Steam the cabbage for 5 minutes, or until it's bright green and beginning to soften.

Meanwhile, melt 125g/4¼oz of the butter in a small saucepan. Remove from the heat and stir in the mace, seaweed flakes and ½ teaspoon of the salt.

Remove the lid (or foil) from the cabbage pan and allow any remaining water in the pan to evaporate. Pour over the melted butter and while still over a high heat, repeatedly tilt the pan towards you to spoon the melted butter over each wedge before returning to the heat. Continue to tilt, baste and cook for 5 minutes before carefully turning the cabbage wedges over and repeating the process on the other cut side (the round exterior should always be facing up). Remove from the heat.

Pour the sherry into the buttery pan and whisk to combine with the remaining cabbage butter. Remove the cabbage from the pan, transfer to an ovenproof serving platter and keep warm in the oven. While the pan is still warm, but not on any heat source, cut the remaining butter into cubes and add a cube at a time to the pan, whisking to melt between each addition. Return the pan to the heat and whisk in the lemon juice and the remaining ½ teaspoon salt. Whisk, while the mixture boils, for 1 minute, or until the sauce thickens to the consistency of single cream.

Pour the seaweed butter over the cabbage and sprinkle over the remaining seaweed flakes. Serve immediately.

Crab, lemon + chilli pasta

Pasta cranc, lemon a tsili

 30 minutes

2 as a main or 4 as a side

A simple dish that tastes like far more than the sum of its parts. The lemon really shines through and elevates the delicate crab to something special. Roasted asparagus makes a very good vegetarian or vegan alternative.

50ml/1¾fl oz extra virgin olive oil
1 banana shallot, finely chopped
1 red chilli, finely chopped
   (seeds and all)
2 garlic cloves, finely sliced
2 lemons
150g/5oz dried linguine
Small bunch of parsley, stalks and
   leaves finely chopped separately
200g/7oz white crab meat
Finer flaked sea salt and freshly
   ground black pepper

Bring a large saucepan of water to the boil. Once it's boiling, add plenty of salt.

Heat the olive oil in a deep frying pan over a medium heat. Add the shallot, chilli, garlic, grated zest of one of the lemons and a pinch of salt and cook, stirring occasionally, for 5 minutes, or until the shallot is soft and translucent and the garlic is starting to turn golden.

Meanwhile, lower the pasta into the boiling water and cook according to the packet instructions.

Cut the two ends off the zested lemon and use a sharp knife to slice off the skin and white pith, leaving just the juicy lemon flesh inside. Cut the lemon into 1cm/½in rounds, discarding the pips as you go, then roughly chop into 1cm/½in pieces. Cut the other lemon into wedges and set aside for serving, if you like. Add the chopped lemon and parsley stalks to the shallot mixture in the pan and stir to combine, then cook for 3–4 minutes, stirring frequently, until the parsley stalks are tender. Add the crab meat and stir to combine, then cook for 2 minutes, or until the crab meat is piping hot. Taste the mixture and add salt and pepper, if you like.

Drain the pasta, reserving 3 tablespoons of the pasta cooking water. Return the pasta to the pan and stir through the pasta cooking water, the vegetable and crab mixture and the chopped parsley leaves. Use tongs to mix everything together until thoroughly combined.

Serve on warmed plates with plenty of black pepper and the reserved lemon wedges for squeezing over, although this is so citrusy you may not need to.

Seaweed rostis

🕐 45 minutes

🍴 2 as a main, or 4 as a side

Seaweed adds a real savoury note to these rostis. Salting the potato first ensures these guys are extra crispy. They are delicious with an egg – poached or fried, your choice – on top at any time of the day

1kg/2lb 3¼oz floury potatoes, such as King Edward or Maris Piper, peeled and roughly grated

1 banana shallot, roughly grated

1 tsp finer flaked sea salt

½ small bunch of parsley, leaves picked and roughly chopped

1 heaped tsp dried seaweed flakes

1 medium egg, beaten

1 heaped tsp plain flour

½ tsp baking powder

Vegetable oil, for frying

Flaked sea salt and freshly ground black pepper

Edible allium flowers (optional), to serve

For the herb salsa

½ small bunch of parsley, finely chopped

½ small bunch of basil, finely chopped

2 tbsp capers in brine, roughly chopped

1 tsp caper brine from the jar

1 garlic clove, grated

60ml/2¼fl oz extra virgin olive oil

Finely grated zest and juice of ½ unwaxed lemon

Preheat the oven to 120°C/100°C fan/250°F/Gas 1.

Put the grated potato and shallot into a large bowl and sprinkle over the finer flaked salt. Using clean hands, rub the salt into the vegetables as though you are rubbing butter into flour for at least 2 minutes until liquid from the vegetables appears in the bowl. Transfer the vegetables to a clean tea towel and gather up the sides, then squeeze the tea towel over the sink to extract as much liquid from the vegetables as possible. Rinse the bowl, wipe dry, then return the squeezed vegetables to the bowl. Add the chopped parsley and seaweed.

Add the beaten egg, flour and baking powder to the bowl, season generously with black pepper and stir to combine.

Heat enough vegetable oil in a large non-stick frying pan to cover the base by 2mm/¹⁄₁₆in over a medium heat. Place a wire rack on a baking sheet nearby and line the rack with kitchen paper. When the oil shimmers in the pan, take heaped tablespoons of the rosti mixture and fry in batches of 3–4 for 4–5 minutes on each side until golden. Make sure there is space between each rosti for flipping and press down on the top of each rosti with the back of a spatula to shape them into even 10cm/4in discs. Transfer the cooked rostis to the lined wire rack to drain. Keep the cooked rostis warm in the oven with the door slightly ajar (this will prevent them going soggy) while you cook the rest and make the salsa, topping up the pan with oil as needed.

To make the herb salsa, stir all the ingredients for the salsa together in a small bowl. Taste and adjust the seasoning with more lemon juice or brine, if you prefer. It should taste punchy, sharp and fresh all at the same time.

Bring a saucepan of water to the boil, add a little salt, then add the kale leaves and blanch for 1 minute. Drain in a colander.

Serve the rostis topped with a spoon of the salsa, a sprinkle of flaked salt and the edible flowers, if using.

The rostis can be made up to 12 hours in advance and reheated in a low oven before serving, but they are best served as soon as they are cooked. The salsa can be covered and stored in the fridge up to three days.

Whipped cod's roe

Grawn penfras wedi'i chwisgio

Wonderful as part of a mezze-type spread, this is our version of a taramasalata and infinitely better than anything you can buy ready-made. You can find smoked cod's roe online if your local fishmonger doesn't supply it. It is naturally very salty, so you may wish to adjust the amount of lemon juice or add a little more water if you prefer a thinner consistency. As an optional extra, this is excellent served with grated cured egg yolk (p.131) on top for added flavour.

 20 minutes

 6–8

4 thick slices of white bread, crusts removed (about 150g/5¼oz prepared weight)
250ml/8½fl oz whole milk
200g/7oz smoked cod's roe
1 garlic clove, grated
125ml/4¼fl oz best extra virgin olive oil, plus extra for drizzling
150ml/5¼fl oz sunflower oil
75ml/2½fl oz ice-cold water
Juice of 1 lemon
2 heaped tbsp full-fat crème fraîche
Pinch of cayenne pepper
Freshly ground black pepper

To serve
Crudités
Pitta bread
Lemon wedges

Put the bread into a large bowl and pour over the milk. Leave to soak for 10 minutes.

Meanwhile, use a sharp knife to split the roe skin down the length of the roe, then use a spoon to scoop out the roe into a food processor. Squeeze out the excess milk from the bread (save the milk for bread sauce or another dish) and add the bread to the processor together with the garlic.

Combine the oils in a large jug and measure the water into a smaller jug. Blitz the roe, bread and garlic together, then with the motor running at medium speed, very slowly pour a quarter of the oils and then a quarter of the water until they are incorporated. Repeat slowly adding the remaining oil and water until both are used up.

Generously season the mixture with pepper, then add the lemon juice and crème fraîche. Scrape down the sides of the food processor and blitz again to combine. Taste the mixture and add more lemon juice if you prefer, or a splash more water if you are aiming for a thinner consistency. Transfer the whipped roe to a serving bowl and ripple a spoon over the top. Drizzle with more olive oil and sprinkle over the cayenne. Serve with the crudités, pitta bread and lemon wedges.

Note
Alternating water and oil to the mixture will stabilise it as it mixes, as well as creating a light texture for this classic dip. When making this in a small food processor, we found that the bread can sometimes clump together. If that happens, remove the lid and scrape down the sides and base with a spatula.

SEASONED
SWEETS + DRINKS

MELYSION A
DIODYDD

Ginger crunch

Anyone familiar with this classic New Zealand biscuit is likely to love it. Don't be fooled by the fairly run-of-the-mill name, this is not a run-of-the-mill traybake. It's a crisp, buttery shortbread with a healthy ratio of wonderfully smooth and very intense, fudgy ginger icing. To take it to the next level, we have added cardamom to our shortbread and finished the icing with smoked sea salt, which complements the ginger perfectly, but if you don't have it, the ginger packs a punch by itself.

For the base

175g/6oz butter, plus extra for greasing

100g/3½oz golden caster sugar

50g/1¾oz light brown sugar

175g/6oz plain flour

2 tsp ground cardamom (about 10 cardamom pods), optional

1½ tsp baking powder

Pinch of finer flaked sea salt

For the icing

125g/4½oz icing sugar, sifted

100g/3½oz butter

2 tbsp golden syrup

4 tsp ground ginger

Flaked smoked sea salt, to finish

🕐 30 minutes

🍴 Makes 12 slices

Preheat the oven to 180°C/160°C fan/350°F/Gas 4. Grease and line a 20cm/8in square baking tin with baking paper.

Using an electric stand mixer with the paddle attachment, cream the butter and sugars together until pale and fluffy. Sift in all the dry ingredients and mix until combined – it will be a very crumbly dough consistency. Scrape the dough into the prepared tin, using your fingers to push it into the corners and make it level. Prick the dough a few times all over with a fork and bake in the oven for about 20 minutes, or until it is a pale gold colour.

When your shortbread has about 10 minutes left, get on with the icing. Heat all the ingredients for the icing gently in a saucepan, stirring to combine. If you didn't sift the icing sugar, you can whisk vigorously to remove any lumps.

Remove the shortbread from the oven and pour the icing over the top while it is still warm. Leave until cool, then leave to set in the fridge for at least 1 hour before cutting. Sprinkle with a good few flakes of smoked salt just before serving.

Two top tips
To measure golden syrup, lightly cover the tablespoon with vegetable oil first. If the cardamom is rather old, toast it slightly before using the pods to release some of the amazing fragrant oils.

Vanilla + raspberry crème brûlée

Crème brûlée fanila a mafon

Prep time: 20 minutes
Cook time: 25 minutes, plus
at least 6 hours chilling

8

Who can resist the satisfying crack of a brûlée, especially when the caramelised crust is balanced with a crunch of sea salt? We make ours in a large dish to share – an impressive centrepiece, but you can make it in individual ramekins using the same method if you prefer. Just remember that it will set more quickly in ramekins. The crème brûlée will set to a custard consistency after about 6 hours, but if you prefer a firmer set then leave it overnight in the fridge.

Butter, for greasing

70g/2¾oz caster sugar, plus 1 tbsp
  for the raspberies

300g/10½oz raspberries

100ml/3½fl oz whole milk

500ml/18fl oz double cream

1 vanilla pod, split in half lengthways

3 bay leaves

6 large egg yolks (or 8 medium egg yolks)

2 tsp cornflour

5 tbsp demerara sugar

Finer flaked sea salt

Lightly grease a round 20cm/8in enamel or ceramic pie dish with butter. Scatter over the tablespoon of the caster sugar and ⅛ teaspoon salt. Roughly crush half the raspberries with the tines of a fork and use the fork to evenly distribute the ruby red berries over the base of the dish. Chill in the freezer.

Pour the milk and cream into a large saucepan and scrape the vanilla seeds into the liquid with the back of a knife. Add the vanilla pod and bay leaves and heat gently over a medium-low heat for 3 minutes, or until the contents of the pan begin to steam and bubbles appear around the sides of the pan. Remove from the heat and set aside.

Whisk the egg yolks, cornflour and the remaining caster sugar together in a large, heatproof bowl until the mixture is light and frothy. Pour over the hot creamy mixture and whisk to combine.

Half-fill a sink with cold water as a precaution when you cook the custard in case it appears as though it might split, which is only likely if the pan gets too hot in places and the custard stirring stops for any length of time.

Pour the custard mixture back into the saucepan you used to heat the cream and cook the custard over a low heat, stirring constantly, for 12–15 minutes until it's thickened to the consistency of natural yogurt. A rubber spatula is best for this to peel away the liquid from the sides and bottom edges of the pan. If it looks as though it's about to split, remove from the heat and plunge into the cold water in the sink, continuing to stir. The custard should look like custard, rather than thick cream by the time you remove it. Remove the vanilla pod and bay leaves from the custard and discard. Remove the dish from the freezer and pour the warm custard over the raspberries. Leave to cool completely, then cover and chill in the fridge for at least 6 hours, or overnight for a firmer set.

When ready to serve, toss the demerara sugar together with ¼ teaspoon of salt in a medium bowl. Scatter the salt and sugar mixture evenly over the surface of the custard, which will still have a slight wobble in the centre when you shake it, then use a blowtorch to melt the sugar-salt crust until the sugar is black in places. Serve immediately with the remaining raspberries.

Toasted milk cookies

Bisgedi llefrith

🕐 Prep time: 10 minutes, plus
3 hours resting +
Cook time: 15 minutes

🍴 Makes 18 cookies

225g/8oz butter
140g/5oz caster sugar
2 medium eggs
2 tsp vanilla extract
50g/1¾oz milk powder
140g/5oz soft dark brown sugar
280g/10oz plain flour
1 tsp bicarbonate of soda
½ tsp finer flaked sea salt
225g/8oz good-quality dark chocolate
  (at least 70% cocoa solids), chopped
Flaked sea salt, for scattering

Note
There are a few stages here,
but the good news is, once
you've made a batch, they freeze
well in individual portions and
you can bake them as and when
needed – just add a couple of
minutes to the cooking time.

This recipe is based on some cookies that Jess had at the wedding of friends, Paddy and Carolyn in upstate New York a few years ago. The groom, a chef, made these with his cousin (also a chef) for the lucky guests. They are the right balance of sweet and salt with an extra toasty depth – the kind of cookie you never want to end. We have adapted the recipe ever so slightly, but the soul remains the same. The depth here comes from two ingredients – brown butter and the secret, toasted whole milk powder. The latter is something you're going to have to seek out, but it's easy to buy good organic stuff online, and trust me, the smell when you open the oven door will be so worth it.

Start by browning the butter. Melt the butter in a small saucepan over a medium heat, then cook until the butter begins to foam and turn a couple of shades darker, tilting and swirling the pan so you can see the butter changing colour as it cooks under the foam. When the butter is browned and smells nutty, about 5 minutes, remove from the heat and use a wooden spoon to loosen the solids from the base of the pan. Browned butter can continue to cook for longer than you think – it's only when it tastes bitter that it has gone too far. Pour the melted butter, bits and all, into a large bowl and leave to cool for an hour or so.

Preheat the oven to 150°C/130°C fan/300°F/Gas 2. Line a large baking sheet with baking paper.

Spread the milk powder over the lined baking sheet in a thin, even layer and toast in the oven until golden. It should take less than 10 minutes, but check every 4 minutes or so as it catches very easily. When golden, leave to cool. If it's clumped up in the oven, smash it into a powder once again.

Using a stand mixer with the balloon whisk attachment, whisk the caster sugar, eggs and vanilla together for 5–10 minutes until thick ribbons of the mixture form when you lift the whisk from the bowl.

Add the cooled, toasted milk powder and the dark brown sugar to the browned butter and roughly mix it together.

Whisk the flour, bicarbonate of soda and finer flaked salt together in another large bowl until combined.

Add the buttery mixture to the egg mixture, a spoonful at a time, and fully incorporate before adding the next one.

If using a freestanding mixer, switch the attachment to the paddle. Add the flour mixture to the wet ingredients in three stages, incorporating the flour until no dry patches are visible with each addition. Add the final third of the flour by hand, together with the chopped chocolate, mixing with a wooden spoon.

Cover the dough and chill in the fridge for at least 2 hours, or overnight. You can keep the dough refrigerated like this for up to three days. If chilling overnight, remove the dough from the fridge 30 minutes before baking.

When ready to bake, preheat the oven to 170°C/150°C fan/ 340°F/Gas 3 and line 2 large baking sheets with baking paper.

Using an ice-cream scoop, scoop 50–60g/1¾ –2½oz rounds from the dough and place on the lined baking sheets, leaving at least 4cm/1½in space between each round to allow for spreading. Bake for 11–15 minutes until they are golden brown but not too crisp. As soon as they come out of the oven, sprinkle a good amount of flaked salt on top and leave to cool on the sheets. Store in an airtight container for a week.

Lemon curd tart with smoked salt shortbread crust

Tarten gaws lemon gyda chrwst bisged Berffro a halen mŵg

Prep time: 25 minutes, plus 1 hour chilling
Cook time: 1 hour 20 minutes, plus 4 hours setting

8

For the pastry
250g/9oz plain flour
125g/4½oz butter, chilled and cubed,
   plus extra for greasing
70g/2½oz icing sugar, sifted
1½ tsp smoked sea salt
1 medium egg, plus 1 egg yolk
1–2 tbsp ice-cold water

For the filling
225g/8oz caster sugar
¼ tsp finer flaked sea salt
Zest of 4 unwaxed lemons,
   plus 115ml/4fl oz juice
   (from about 4–5 lemons)
4 medium eggs
125ml/4¼fl oz double cream
100g/3½oz butter, cubed
20g/¾oz icing sugar (optional)

This classic dessert is lifted by the smoky edge in the shortbread crust. If you're feeling fancy, then you can finish it beautifully with a quick brûlée topping. Life doesn't get much better than a slice of this with a spoonful of seasonal berries.

To make the pastry, pulse the flour, butter, icing sugar and smoked salt in a food processor until the mixture resembles breadcrumbs. Add the whole egg (not the extra yolk) and pulse again to combine. Pour in the water, 1 tablespoon at a time, until the mixture comes together when you pinch it between your fingers. You may not need all the water. The dough will be crumbly, but bring it together into a disc, roughly 12cm/4½in in diameter. Cover in clingfilm and chill in the fridge for 1 hour.

Meanwhile, make a start on the lemon curd. Measure the caster sugar and salt into a large heatproof bowl. Add the zest to the bowl, and, using clean hands, rub the mixture together until the sugar no longer looks dry and begins to clump together. This will extract the aromatic oil from the lemon skin, intensifying the lemon flavour. Cover and set aside.

Preheat the oven to 180°C/160°C fan/350°F/Gas 4. Grease a 23cm/9in loose-bottomed tart tin with butter.

Remove the pastry from the fridge and, using clean hands, push the crumbly tart dough into the base and sides of the prepared tin, coming up to 1cm/½in above the rim. As it is a shortbread dough, rather than a classic pastry base, it may feel a little 'rustic', but persist in pressing and shaping the dough to fill the tin evenly. Prick the base of the pastry all over with a fork, then cover with baking paper, making sure some of the paper hangs over the side. Fill with baking beans and blind bake in the oven for 10 minutes. Remove the beans and paper and bake for another 10 minutes, or until golden brown all over.

Remove from the oven, lightly beat the remaining egg yolk in a small bowl and brush the base all over with the yolk. Return to the oven for another minute. Remove from the oven and reduce the oven temperature to 150°C/130°C fan/300°F/Gas 2.

For the filling, crack the eggs into the bowl with the lemon sugar mixture and pour in the cream and 115ml/4fl oz lemon juice from the zested lemons. Whisk to combine. Set the bowl over a saucepan of simmering water, making sure the base of the bowl doesn't touch the surface of the water, and cook, stirring frequently and maintaining the heat so the water is at a simmer for 12–14 minutes until the custard has thickened to coat the back of a wooden spoon. Remove from the heat and leave to cool for 2 minutes before whisking in the cubed butter, two pieces at a time, until melted and combined.

Pour the custard into the tart crust and bake in the oven for about 22–25 minutes until just set but with a distinct wobble in the centre. Leave to cool at room temperature for 1 hour before transferring to the fridge for at least 4 hours, or overnight until completely set.

If finishing with the brûlée topping, dredge the top of the set tart with the icing sugar and carefully heat with a blowtorch until all the sugar is melted, bubbling and burnt in places. The tart will keep covered in the fridge for up to three days.

Dark chocolate + rum truffle tart

Tarten siocled tywyll a rym

This tart is incredibly easy to make, but tastes and looks as impressive as the finest French patisserie (OK, nearly). The contrast between the thin crisp base and the rich chocolate ganache is what makes it a winner, with the flaked sea salt really cuts through the richness at the end.

100g/3½oz butter, at room temperature, plus extra for greasing
200g/7oz plain tuile biscuits (sometimes sold as cigar or cigarette biscuits)
1 tbsp cocoa powder
350ml/12⅓fl oz double cream
300g/10½oz dark chocolate (at least 70% cocoa solids), finely chopped
50g/1¾oz milk chocolate, finely chopped
1 tsp vanilla bean paste
40ml/1½fl oz dark rum
Finer flaked and flaked sea salt

To serve
Crème fraîche
Fresh mixed berries

 Time taken: 45 minutes, plus 90 minutes chilling

 10

Preheat the oven to 180°C/160°C fan/350°F/Gas 4. Lightly grease the base and sides of a 23cm/9in loose-bottomed tart tin with butter and line the base of the tin with baking paper.

Pulse the biscuits, cocoa powder and a pinch of fine salt together in a food processor until a fine crumb forms, then transfer to a large bowl.

Melt 50g/1¾oz of the butter in a small saucepan, then pour it over the biscuit mixture and stir until the mixture is combined and resembles wet sand. Using a clean, flat-bottomed glass, pack the biscuit mixture evenly into the prepared tin, shaping it around the sides so that it meets the rim at the top all around the edge. Bake the biscuit case in the oven for 10–12 minutes until it starts to look darker around the top. Leave to cool completely.

Meanwhile, pour the cream into a medium saucepan, leaving at least 5cm/2in of space between the surface of the cream and the top of the pan and heat until you see bubbles start to form around the side of the pan. Remove from the heat and scatter both chocolates over the cream so that it covers as much of the surface of the cream as possible, rather than forming a pile in the centre. Leave for 1 minute without stirring, then stir to combine. The mixture should be thick and glossy. Cut the remaining 50g/1¾oz butter into six pieces and whisk into the chocolate mixture, a piece at a time, until smooth. Stir in the vanilla and rum, then pour the chocolate mixture into the prepared tin, without letting any spill over the sides of the biscuit case. Shake the tin gently to distribute the chocolate filling evenly, then chill in the fridge for 90 minutes.

Remove the tart from the fridge and scatter over a generous pinch of flaked salt (any earlier and the salt will sink into the chocolate mixture). Chill for at least another hour, or up to 24 hours before slicing. Serve with crème fraîche and fresh berries. The tart will keep covered in the fridge for up to three days.

No-churn hazelnut espresso ice cream

Hufen iâ espresso cnau cyll

This is an absolute knockout ice cream with no need for an ice-cream maker, or checking the freezer every 30 minutes. Miraculous. The nuts are toasted when they are the colour of milky coffee rather than butter – this will release the aromatic oils in the hazelnuts and, along with the sea salt, will really intensify the flavour of the ice cream. Delicious on its own, or served alongside a good slice of Ginger Crunch (p.195) or Dark Chocolate and Rum Truffle Tart (p.205).

425ml/15fl oz double cream

1 tsp finer flaked or smoked sea salt

½ tsp vanilla bean paste

50g/1¾oz hazelnuts, toasted

397g/14oz tin sweetened condensed milk

125ml/4¼fl oz very strong coffee or espresso, cooled

🕐 15 minutes, plus 8 hours freezing

🍴 6

Using an electric whisk, beat the cream, salt and vanilla together in a large bowl until the mixture resembles natural yogurt.

Rub the toasted hazelnuts together in a clean tea towel to remove as much of their skins as possible. Discard the papery skins and roughly chop the nuts. Set aside a tablespoon or so to sprinkle over the top, then add most of the nuts, the condensed milk and cooled coffee to the cream mix and beat together until it thickens to the consistency of natural yogurt. Pour the mixture into a 900g/2lb loaf tin, sprinkle over the reserved hazelnuts and cover with clingfilm. Chill in the freezer for at least 8 hours, or overnight.

Remove the ice cream from the freezer 5 minutes before serving. The ice cream will keep covered in the freezer for three months.

Salted honey brittle

Alison's father Ian travelled all around the world for his work, believe it or not, selling fire engines. (Decades later, Alison would win the same Queen's award for salt as he did for selling his beloved fire engines.) Ian would come back home laden with exotic sweets, and Alison's favourites were always sesame snaps. This brittle is rather like a posh version of those childhood favourites. Look for black sesame seeds online or in larger supermarkets, but if you can't find them, use double the amount of the white ones instead.

250g/9oz runny honey
75g/2¾oz shelled pistachio nuts, roughly chopped
25g/1oz black sesame seeds
25g/1oz sesame seeds
1 tsp smoked or flaked sea salt
½ tsp vanilla bean paste

Prep time: 5 minutes
Cook time: 10 minutes, plus 1 hour setting

10–12

Line a baking sheet with baking paper or a silicone mat and set aside until needed.

Pour the honey into a medium saucepan, leaving at least 6cm/2½in of space between the surface of the honey and the top of the pan. Clip a sugar thermometer onto the side of the pan and bring the honey to the boil over a medium-high heat for 8 minutes, or until it reaches 148°C/298°F, or the 'hard crack' stage.

Meanwhile, measure all the remaining ingredients together into a large, heatproof bowl.

When the honey comes to temperature, remove from the heat and, working quickly but calmly, immediately pour onto the pistachio mixture in the bowl. Stir with a spatula to combine, then tip everything onto the prepared baking sheet and use the spatula to spread it out so the mixture is roughly 3mm/⅛in thick. Leave to set at room temperature for 1 hour.

Use a small hammer or clean hands to break the brittle into irregular pieces and store in an airtight container for up to five days.

Ideas for serving:

• Sprinkle small shards on top of vanilla ice cream.
• Finely chop and stir into crème fraîche to decorate a fruity tart (see the Lemon Curd Tart on p.201).
• Serve alongside coffee.
• Sprinkle on top of a Victoria sponge cake or cream puddings for a crunchy contrast.
• Chop very finely and sprinkle on top of roasted squash or carrots to serve as an indulgent savoury side.
• Wrap a few pieces in baking paper and give as edible gifts.

Scotch caramels

Whisky and smoked salt go together beautifully, and this caramel offers the perfect foundation for both flavours to really sing. Little squares of balanced sweet and salty joy. Like all sugar work, these caramels demand accuracy to prevent the risk of the sweets not setting, or becoming tooth-shatteringly hard, you will need a sugar thermometer to ensure they heat to the right temperature. Wrapped in squares of baking paper, these caramels make great gifts on their own.

Sunflower oil, for oiling
175g/6oz caster sugar
5 tbsp golden syrup (about 100g/3½oz)
125g/4½oz butter
250ml/9fl oz double cream
½ tsp finer flaked sea salt
3 tbsp Scotch whisky
1 tsp flaked salt or flaked smoked salt

Prep time: 5 minutes
Cook time: 30 minutes, plus overnight setting

Makes 36 squares

Lightly oil a 20cm/8in square baking tin and line with baking paper that is long and wide enough to reach all the top edges of the tin.

Pour the caster sugar, golden syrup and 3 tablespoons water into a deep, medium saucepan. Clip a sugar thermometer onto the side of the pan, then heat over a low-medium heat, stirring occasionally with a spatula, for 6–8 minutes until the sugar is dissolved and the mixture is liquid.

Gently melt the butter in a small saucepan and stir in the cream. Keep the mixture warm over a low heat.

Increase the heat on the sugar pan to medium-high and boil the sugar mixture for another 5–7 minutes until the sugar reaches 155°C/311°F, brushing any visible white sugar crystals from the side of the pan with a wet pastry brush to prevent crystallisation of the caramel later.

Remove the molten sugar from the heat and pour in the warm cream mixture in three stages, stirring between each addition and taking care as the hot caramel mixture will quickly bubble up the sides of the pan. When all the cream mixture has been stirred into the sugar, return the pan to the heat and cook, stirring frequently with a spatula, until the thermometer reaches 122°C/252°F, or 130°C/266°F if you prefer a firmer set.

Working quickly, but confidently and calmly, remove the pan from the heat and add the finer flaked salt. Stir in the whisky in three stages, taking care as it will boil furiously with each addition. Stir to combine, then pour into the prepared tin and leave to set for 10 minutes before scattering over the flaked salt. Cover and leave to set at room temperature, ideally overnight, before cutting into 36 squares with a lightly oiled sharp knife.

Wrap the salted caramels in squares of baking paper and eat within a week. Alternatively, the caramels can be frozen for up to three months before consuming. Defrost them completely before serving.

Salted caramel apple bread + butter pudding

Pwdin bara menyn afal a charamel môr

This dessert is everything one could want from a pudding and more – sweet and salty, creamy and comforting and the culinary equivalent of a deep, warm bath. This recipe makes extra salted caramel, which will keep well in the fridge for a few days. Use it sandwiched in a pavlova, poured over ice cream, stirred through porridge or even, as Jake discovered recently, cheer up elevenses by adding a spoonful to your coffee.

 1 hour 45 minutes

4–6

For the apple sauce
3 large eating apples, peeled, cored and cubed

For the salted caramel sauce
175g/6oz soft light brown sugar
300ml/10½fl oz double cream
50g/1¾oz butter
¼ tsp finer flaked sea salt

For the pudding
50g1¾oz butter, softened, plus extra for greasing
6 slices of brioche bread, from a 400g/14oz loaf, preferably stale
3 medium eggs
500ml/18fl oz whole milk
50g/1¾oz soft light brown sugar
1 tbsp demerara sugar, for sprinkling
Pouring cream, crème fraîche or Hazelnut Espresso Ice Cream (p.208), to serve

Preheat the oven to 180°C/160°C fan/350°F/Gas 4. Generously grease a deep, heatproof baking dish, about 16 x 21cm/6½ x 8½in, with butter.

Make the apple sauce. Place the prepared apples and 2 tablespoons water in a medium saucepan and simmer gently, stirring frequently, over a low heat until soft. Using a stick blender, purée the apples, leaving some texture, if you prefer, then leave to cool.

Next, make the salted caramel sauce. Melt all the ingredients in a medium saucepan over a low heat, stirring until the sugar has dissolved. Let the sauce bubble until it thickens and turns golden brown. Leave to cool (it will thicken), then ripple two-thirds of the sauce through the apple purée. Set aside and store the remaining apple sauce in the fridge. It is wonderful poured over ice cream, stirred through porridge or sandwiched in a pavlova.

To assemble the pudding, butter the brioche slices generously, then cut them into four triangles per slice.

Beat the eggs, milk and light brown sugar together in another bowl until combined.

Stack the bread in the prepared dish so that the slices overlap. Dot in between with the apple and caramel sauce until it is all used up, then pour over the custard mixture. Sprinkle the top with the demerara sugar and bake for 45–55 minutes until the pudding is lightly set and golden brown. Serve warm with pouring cream, crème fraîche or ice cream.

Grapefruit + ginger treacle tarts

Tartenni triog grawnffrwyth a sinsir

Treacle tart is one of life's pleasures, reminiscent of Sunday evenings in our house. This recipe pairs the classic flavours of ginger and grapefruit and sets them against the richness of golden syrup and a crisp, buttery pastry.

For the pastry

250g/9oz plain flour

½ tsp finer flaked sea salt

140g/5oz butter, chilled and cut into cubes

2 tbsp icing sugar, sifted

2 medium egg yolks

1–2 tbsp ice-cold water

For the filling

400g/14oz golden syrup

2 balls stem ginger in syrup, finely chopped

50ml/1¾fl oz ginger syrup

Finely grated zest of 1 red or ruby grapefruit

2 medium eggs, lightly beaten

100g/3½oz white or brown breadcrumbs

Flaked sea salt, to finish

Prep time: 30 minutes, plus chilling
Cook time: 45 minutes

Makes 12 mini tarts

To make the pastry, sift the flour into a large bowl, add the salt and rub in the butter until it looks like breadcrumbs. This can be done by hand or in a food processor. Stir in the icing sugar, then add the egg yolks and water and mix until the dough comes together, adding more water, a little at a time, if needed. Form the pastry into a ball, wrap in clingfilm and chill in the fridge for 30 minutes.

Once the pastry is chilled, roll it out to about 5mm/¼in thick. Use a cutter just larger than the indentations of the tin, to cut out rounds and fill the holes of a 12-hole non-stick muffin tray. Line with baking paper, cover and chill for 30 minutes.

Meanwhile, preheat the oven to 200°C/180°C fan/400°F/Gas 6.

Cover the pastry with round of baking paper and fill with baking beans, then blind bake in the oven for 10 minutes. Remove the beans and paper and bake for another 5–10 minutes until the pastry is golden brown. Remove from the oven and reduce the oven temperature to 160°C/140°C fan/325°F/Gas 3.

To make the filling, put all the filling ingredients into a large bowl and mix well until combined. Pour the filling into the pastry cases and bake for 35–40 minutes until the filling is just set. Leave to cool to room temperature, then scatter over a few flakes of sea salt before serving.

Note
The recipe works well if you prefer to use 12cm/4½in tart tins for larger tarts. They will yield about nine of these. Prepare as above, but the bake may take a couple of minutes longer.

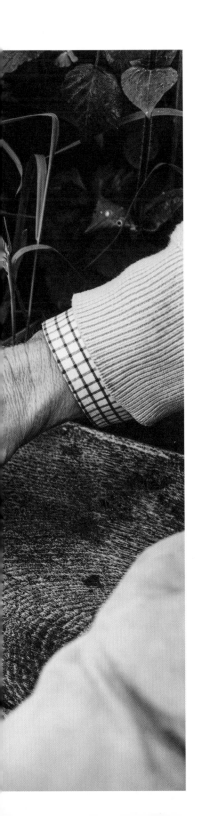

Campfire latte

Latte coelcerth

This blend of coffee, maple syrup and smoked sea salt has been a bestseller on the menu of our outdoor café ever since we opened. In the summer we have a tipi at our Saltcote, and sipping one of these sitting under the canvas, brings back memories of campfires of our childhood. Pure nostalgia. We have Scott to thank for this recipe. He started and owns a genuinely inspirational business, Coaltown Coffee, in South Wales. We recommend you seek out his beans of Black Gold, which we use in the café and adore.

20g (¾oz) ground Coaltown Coffee: Black Gold No.3
1 tsp maple syrup
225ml/8fl oz milk or milk alternative
Pinch of smoked sea salt

Prepare a double shot of espresso according to the machine's instructions, then stir in a good teaspoon of maple syrup. Steam the milk using your machine and pour gently onto the espresso. Finish with the smoked salt.

Salted caramel hot chocolate

Siocled poeth caramel môr

A rich hot chocolate paired with the unbeatable flavour of salted caramel.

200ml/7fl oz milk or milk alternative
25g/1oz good-quality milk chocolate, grated
    (we like Pump Street sourdough and sea salt bar)
2 tsp Salted Caramel Sauce (p.215)
1 tbsp cocoa powder
Finer flaked sea salt, to taste
Sugar, to taste (optional)

Heat the milk gently in a large saucepan until simmering, being careful not to let it catch on the base of the pan. Remove from the heat and stir in the chocolate until melted. Return to the hob and add the caramel sauce and cocoa. Taste and add a pinch of salt and sugar, if you like. Pour into a mug and enjoy.

Spicy ginger iced tea

Te sinsir sbeislyd oer

 5 minutes, plus 1–6 hours standing

Makes 1 litre/35fl oz

This sunny tea can be drunk hot or cold, topped up with sparkling water or even knocked back in an ice-cold shot to put the pep back in your step. Using a little salt magically helps draw out the punchy flavours. Having black pepper and turmeric together apparently magnifies the health benefits of both, but, if your body is more of an 'amusement park'* than a temple, this drink also makes a beautiful base for a rum or whisky cocktail.

150g/5¼oz fresh root ginger
40g/1½oz fresh turmeric root
150g/5¼oz caster sugar
1 tsp finer flaked sea salt
1 litre/35fl oz strong redbush tea made
  with 3 tea bags
100ml/3½fl oz freshly squeezed lemon
  juice (about 2–3 lemons), plus lemon
  slices to garnish
Sparkling water (optional)
Freshly ground black pepper

Roughly grate the ginger and turmeric (there's no need to peel either) into a bowl on the large setting of a box grater. Toss with the sugar, salt and pepper from about 10 turns of the pepper mill. Cover and set aside at room temperature for at least 1 hour, or up to 6 hours for a stronger flavour.

Pour the ginger mixture into the centre of a muslin cloth draped over the top of a large (1.5 litre/40fl oz) jug. Gather up the sides and squeeze gently to extract as much of the liquid as possible. Discard the grated ginger and turmeric (or save and add to a smoothie). Pour the tea and lemon juice over the ginger liquid and stir to combine. Add a little more lemon to taste if you prefer a sharper drink. Keep covered in the fridge until ready to serve (it can be made up to 24 hours before serving).

When ready to serve, fill a few glasses with ice cubes and pour over the iced tea. If you prefer a sparkling drink, top with 100ml/3½fl oz sparkling water per glass. Garnish with a slice of lemon and serve immediately.

* favourite quote from one of the greats, Anthony Bourdain.

Cherry + black pepper shrub

Sirop ceirios a phupur du

🕐 Prep time: 20 minutes, plus
3 hours macerating +
2 days fermenting

🍴 Makes about 550ml/
19 fl oz

For many years we have worked on products with two recipe developers who have the most discerning tastebuds. Over one memorable meal, they shared with us a food philosophy that has stayed with me (Jess). In their opinion, a recipe should only serve to celebrate the purity of an ingredient – you should only make a drink of cherries if you think it will be better than a cherry straight off the tree, for example. This shrub, we believe, does celebrate the very essence of this fruit, so Brandt and Micah – here's to you.

A shrub, sometimes referred to as a drinking vinegar, adds depth and interest to cocktails, whether boozy or not. Top up with ice-cold soda water, or add a shot of shrub to juice for an added boost. Use ripe or just overripe fruit here – in winter we like rhubarb, or strawberries in early summer, and experiment with herbs, spices and even edible petals for different colours and flavours. Macerating the cherries with salt and sugar at the beginning of the recipe really amplifies their flavour.

500g/1lb 2oz fresh cherries, pitted
215g/7¼oz caster sugar
1 tsp finer flaked sea salt
¾ tsp coarsely cracked black pepper
4 rosemary stalks
215ml/7¼fl oz live apple cider vinegar

Put the cherries, sugar and salt into a large bowl and toss together to combine. Cover with a clean tea towel and leave at room temperature for 3 hours.

Meanwhile, sterilise a 1 litre/35fl oz kilner jar and add the pepper to the jar when cool. Smack the rosemary between the palms of your hands to release its fragrance and add the stalks to the jar with the pepper.

Use a spatula to transfer the cherries, sugar and any juice to the jar, seal with the lid and leave in the fridge for at least 16 hours, or up to 24 hours, shaking the jar a couple of times to help the sugar dissolve.

Remove the jar from the fridge and pour in the vinegar. Keep the jar in a cool place (in the fridge is fine), shaking twice over 24 hours.

Pour the liquid through a clean muslin cloth into a sieve suspended over a bowl, then pour into a large (at least 600ml/20fl oz) sterilised jar or bottle using a funnel and keep sealed in the fridge for up to six months. Once opened, consume within eight weeks.

DIY Bloody Mary with Welsh rarebit

Mari Waedlyd gyda rarebit Cymreig

For the rarebit
½ tsp Dijon mustard
25ml/1fl oz Welsh ale
  (leftover from the night before)
15g/½oz butter
100g/3½oz Cheddar cheese, grated
1 medium egg yolk
Handful of snipped chives
1 tsp smoked water (optional)
2 thick slices of sourdough
Finer flaked sea salt and freshly
  ground black pepper

For the Bloody Mary
100ml/3½fl oz good-quality vodka
400ml/14fl oz tomato juice
Pinch of celery salt
Cracked black pepper
Ice cubes

To garnish
Lemon wedge
Celery stick

Optional add-ins to taste
Dry sherry
Smoked water
Worcestershire sauce
Brine from any jar of olives or pickle
Tabasco sauce
Creamed horseradish

 30 minutes

 2

The Bloody Mary is a classic cocktail for a reason – the perfect way to recover from a rather festive evening the night before. We've provided the ideal base for the cocktail and suggested plenty of optional extras, to keep things interesting. The golden rule is to use the best vodka you can buy. It seems that the garnish of the Bloody Mary has become integral to the drink itself – depending on where you are, your drink may be served with a lobster claw, a serious chunk of cheese or a sizeable gherkin. In our house, of course, there is always celery salt, but when time is on our side, we go all in and serve the drink with little fingers of Welsh rarebit. It's a winning combination of dreamy cheese on toast and a deep, savoury tomato juice.

For the rarebit, preheat the grill to medium. Mix the mustard and ale together in a small saucepan over a low heat, then stir in the butter to melt. Add the Cheddar and stir until the cheese is just melted. Do not let it boil. Remove the pan from the heat and fold in the egg yolk, chives, smoked water, if using, and a pinch of salt and black pepper.

Toast the bread under the grill on both sides, then turn your grill up to its highest setting. Arrange the toasted bread snugly on a baking sheet and divide the rarebit mixture between the two slices (don't worry about it spilling over the edges of the bread). Grill until golden and bubbling.

Make the cocktail by pouring all the ingredients into a cocktail shaker, and pouring from one half to the other rather than shaking. Pour over plenty of ice and garnish with a squeeze of lemon, a celery stick and serve with any of the add-ins listed above, each added to taste.

Frozen blood orange Margarita

Margarita oren coch drwy rew

🕐 5 minutes, plus 4 hours freezing

🍴 Makes 4 large glasses

An absolutely excellent cocktail to create some summer magic even on those darkest of winter days – deliciously balanced and a very pleasing colour. Blood oranges work so well here, but if they are not in season, then use a different freshly squeezed orange juice. The key to a good cocktail, as is the key to much good food, is to keep tasting and adjusting.

For the cocktail
400ml/14fl oz blood orange juice, frozen
120ml/4 fl oz good-quality tequila
85ml/3fl oz triple sec
60ml/2¼fl oz fresh lime juice
A few drops of vanilla extract
Ice cubes

For the glasses
Finer flaked sea salt
Brown sugar
  (smoked for the next level)
½ lime

Pour all the ingredients for the cocktail into a large bowl with a spout or a jug, then whizz it in a blender in two batches.

To serve, sprinkle the salt and sugar onto a small, flat plate. Rub the edge of each glass with the lime, then dip the rim into the salty sugar mix to coat. Pour the cocktail into the glasses and serve immediately.

Note
To add that extra-slushy luxury cocktail level, freeze the blood orange juice in an ice-cube tray before making the cocktail. Alternatively, just use plenty of extra ice.

Index

Afterword

We've been closely involved with sea and food since we were students in Bangor forty-five years ago. An early memory is selling seafood in the Students Union to supplement Alison's grant – lecturers bought the oysters and students bought the mackerel!

We began with a friend as oyster growers, then became wholesale fishmongers supplying many hotels and restaurants in North Wales. Next was a fish stall called Sea Catch and Carry (and a public aquarium). Out of that came the learned craft of making sea salt. The eureka moment was in Japan where I found a museum of salt and a culture that valued sea salt. I re-learned a craft that existed on Anglesey until 1775. Growing that fledgling business with our teams for the last twenty something years has been an exciting and eventful journey and our three children are now even more passionate than we are about food.

I'm really excited to have provided all the sea salt for this book and many of the vegetables. The vegetables came when we moved a mile inland and attached to the derelict house was a derelict walled garden. I believe maximum flavour and 'terroir' or 'merroir ' are found when we use the resources closest to us.

We have a bulging shelf of cookbooks we have learned from and been influenced by. The ones that stick with me most are where the cooking and inspiration is linked to a sense of place either in physical origin or a specific culture. We have tried to follow this ethos. This book very much comes out of Wales – more specifically, from the magical island of *Ynys Môn*/Anglesey – albeit with the enrichment of foods from hotter places.

Anglesey has been known for centuries as *Môn Mam Cymru* – the 'Mother of Wales' – simply because its seas and fertile land used to feed much of mountainous North Wales. The island used to have over one hundred wind and watermills, fields of corn and a sea salt industry. Recently, we have seen the return of a working windmill and a project to reintroduce heritage crops on the island. Our contribution has been to reintroduce the craft of sea salt making for which the island was once well known. One part of Anglesey to this day is known as Salt Island even if it is now the main ferry terminal for Ireland.

As we finish this book the Climate Emergency is increasingly in our minds. We need to not just talk about eating local but actually put this into practice. Seasonality and seasoning are the order of the day. Where we can, we all have a responsibility to use what grows where we live, to celebrate the seasons by eating what is abundant each month, and saving some for leaner months – often using salt. Our pantry is nearly as important as the kitchen. Knowing how to use seasoning properly is a huge part of cooking, and can lift any meal from average to extraordinary. Often less is more whether it is the number of ingredients or even the sea salt you use. In the circular, sustainable economy we strive for, the soil and compost heap are key and even the sea salt co-product is steam from which we extract heat, leaving just distilled water.

If I have just one request, it is to read carefully the origin of the ingredients you use – it is not enough to assume that a product, whether salt or seasoning, with a place name attached means that it actually comes from there! Anglesey Sea Salt means it 100 per cent comes from there – no additional brines from other waters, or other salt or rock salt filters are used – the only ingredient is Anglesey Sea Water. This is the reason we have been awarded the highest accolade for food from the EU and now the UK. We are the UK's sixtieth product with a Designated Origin (PDO). To be place oriented in the same way as Champagne or Melton Mowbray Pork Pie is something we are proud of and won't change.

The book has been a real family project, that we have been working on – testing, eating, cooking and planning for more than a year, although the unconscious research has been going on around our kitchen table for most of our lives. Thank you, Alison, for putting the food on that table for so long and so well.

David Lea-Wilson, MBE, Co-founder of Halen Môn

Thanks

Sometimes you read a mile-long thank you page for a book and think to yourself 'were all of those people really crucial in bringing that book to life?'

The answer, in this case, is a resounding yes.

Thank you to each and every person who helped make this book happen – we know we will have forgotten someone but it doesn't mean we aren't grateful!

Halen Môn

To all of the staff at Halen Môn, who make an incredible product and make it a joy to go to work (most!) of the time.

To all of our customers and suppliers at Halen Môn, all over the world, where we have often found real friendship over the years.

Publishers

To Melissa, who is the main reason this book is in your hands right now. Thank you for believing that our brilliantly chaotic family could pull it off. Thank you Charlotte for your careful guidance too.

To Jessica, thanks for being a voice of calm encouragement throughout.

Isabel, for entrusting Jess' marbling skills to the cover, and for designing a corker of a book.

Liz and Lewis, for their work promoting the book.

To the talented and generous ceramicists who loaned us some incredible pieces for this book

Chloe Rosetta Bell
Liv Vidal
Andrea Roman
Libby Ballard
Lora Wyn (via Nick Rudge!)
Rachael Pilston naturally dyed napkins
Tim Lake

Food producers

Isle of Wight tomato company
Menai Oysters / Hooton's Homegrown
Fish for Thought / Piper's Farm
Belazu / Hawkshead Relish Company
Willy's Apple Cider Vinegar

People

Miriam Leece, Jaya Chandna, Anju Chandna, Jen Shipley, David Gibbon, Andrew Hewitt, Jilly Douglas, Alex Flowers. Thank you for your honest feedback and many hours at the stove on our behalf.

To Josie Hearnden and Elly Kemp, for their excellent recipe testing, and being as appreciative of good food as any Lea-Wilson.

Shane Edward Lyons, whose enthusiasm and love of both food and Wales mean we are very much cut from the same cloth.

Paddy O'Grady whose cookies are the very best we've tasted.

Sam Lomas, who, among many other things, gave us a restaurant experience at home every Friday in lockdown, and knows what he's doing when it comes to an almond croissant.

Anna Jones, for your friendship, encouragement and simply incredible ways with vegetables.

Eamon Fullalove, for so much enthusiasm so early on in our writing career.

Becky, whose contribution and kindness is invaluable to our family.

Richard and Janet whose green fingers simply make our Anglesey garden the magic place it is.

Liz and Max, who take the most beautiful photographs and make every single shoot day one full of happiness and laughter. Coco, we missed you!

And to Anna Shepherd, whose ideas, words and love can be found on every page of this book. We are so lucky that you worked with us on it - thank you.

And finally, to Fyfe and Rupert, the next generation of food lovers.